-THE-
WILD
WORLD
HANDBOOK

How Adventurers, Artists,
Scientists—And You—Can Protect
Earth's Habitats

By Andrea Debbink

Illustrated by Asia Orlando

QUIRK BOOKS
PHILADELPHIA

OTHER BOOKS BY ANDREA DEBBINK

Spark: A Guide to Ignite the Creativity Inside You

Think for Yourself: The Ultimate Guide to
Critical Thinking in an Age of Information Overload

Library of Congress Cataloging in Publication Data

Debbink, Andrea, author. | Orlando, Asia, illustrator.

The wild world handbook : how adventurers, artists, scientists-and you-can protect earth's habitats / by Andrea Debbink ; illustrated by Asia Orlando.

Summary: "A middle-grade guide to environmental stewardship and protecting diverse habitats"—Provided by publisher.

LCSH: Habitat conservation—Juvenile literature. | Habitat (Ecology)—Juvenile literature.

LCC QH75 .D389 2021 | DDC 333.95/16—dc23 2020052824

ISBN: 978-1-68369-246-1

Printed in China

Typeset in Argone, Hawkes, MVB Dovetail, and DTL Nobel

Designed by Elissa Flanigan

Illustrations by Asia Orlando and Elissa Flanigan

Production management by John J. McGurk

Quirk Books
215 Church Street
Philadelphia, PA 19106
quirkbooks.com

10 9 8 7 6 5 4 3 2 1

For Peter,
who shares my wonder
for the wild world

CONTENTS

INTRODUCTION
THE WORLD OUTSIDE

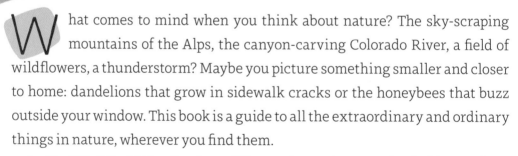

W hat comes to mind when you think about nature? The sky-scraping mountains of the Alps, the canyon-carving Colorado River, a field of wildflowers, a thunderstorm? Maybe you picture something smaller and closer to home: dandelions that grow in sidewalk cracks or the honeybees that buzz outside your window. This book is a guide to all the extraordinary and ordinary things in nature, wherever you find them.

In *The Wild World Handbook*, you'll learn about nine amazing habitats—from polar lands where the sun sometimes shines all day, and sometimes not at all, to mysterious rainforests that are still full of secrets. You'll read stories about natural wonders like the tallest tree in the world and deserts that bloom so bright you can see them from space.

You'll also read stories about people, because people have the power to hurt nature or to help it—and you do, too. The people in this book had incredible experiences in nature and then they did something about it. They're scientists and activists, but they're also photographers, writers, athletes, and explorers. Each of them started out just like you—an ordinary kid—but their actions changed the natural world for the better and helped us understand our place in it.

You probably know this by now: humans have done a lot to hurt nature and the habitats that make up our beautiful, wild world. And we still do. We cut down forests in unsustainable ways, pour pollution into waterways, and take more than we need from the earth. Today we're facing a lot of big environmental challenges as a result of people's actions, such as plant and animal extinction, plastic pollution, and melting glaciers. And all these problems are made worse by climate change and its effects. It can be sad, and scary, to think about all this destruction.

That's why it's helpful—and hopeful—to think about these things, too: There are birds that fly in our skies today because someone a hundred years ago cared enough to protect them. There are forests growing tall because someone planted seedlings. There are rivers with cleaner water and healthy fish because someone cleaned them up. History is full of people who destroyed nature *and* history is full of people who protected and cared for it. Each generation had a choice and we do too: Will we destroy nature and use it up until it's gone? Or will we take care of our world's incredible habitats and help them thrive?

You don't have to be a scientist or a park ranger or a politician or an adult to explore nature or to protect it. You don't have to live in the woods or even like to camp. You don't have to own hiking boots or look a certain way or be from a certain place. There are many ways to explore nature and there are many ways to take care of it. This book will show you how.

-CHAPTER 1-
MOUNTAINS

Mountains can be soft and green or sharp with rock and ice. They can be places of shelter and rest, or they can divide communities with high ridges that are impossible to cross. Mountains are powerful enough to control weather, storing up rain or letting it go. Yet mountain habitats are also fragile enough to be broken apart by explosives or trampled by careless human feet that stray from hiking trails.

The mountains are calling. Let's go.

»» MOUNTAIN FACTS «««

 1. Except for Antarctica, every continent on Earth has at least **50** mountain ranges.

 2. The highest mountains on each of the seven continents are called the Seven Summits: **MOUNT EVEREST** (Asia), **ACONCAGUA** (South America), **DENALI** (North America), **KILIMANJARO** (Africa), **MOUNT ELBRUS** (Europe), **MOUNT VINSON** (Antarctica), and **MOUNT KOSCIUSZKO** (Australia).

 3. Most of the world's rivers begin in the glaciers and snowfields on mountain peaks. Eighty percent of the world's freshwater comes from these mountain rivers.

 4. The longest mountain range on earth is underwater. It's called the mid-ocean ridge and it's more than **40,000** miles long!

 5. People sometimes disagree on the definition of a mountain, but most geologists define a mountain as a landform that's at least **1,000** feet above the land that surrounds it.

THE BRAVE MOUNTAINEER
JUNKO TABEI

SEPTEMBER 22, 1939–OCTOBER 20, 2016

"When people meet me for the first time, they are surprised by my size. They expect me to be bigger than I am, more strapping, robust, like a wrestler for example. As I am the first woman to climb Mount Everest and the Seven Summits, they equate a certain body type to my accomplishments."

—Junko Tabei

From the top of the hill, Junko could see her whole world: her village, the river that flowed past her house, and the Buddhist temples that glowed like flame-colored castles in the sunset. She liked to pretend the largest temple was home to the Japanese emperor.

Junko was small for her age and often sick with illnesses like pneumonia. Even now, another rattling sickness in her lungs made it hard to breathe as she climbed the hill. People said Junko was weak, even fragile. But one day, she would prove them wrong.

First Summit

Junko Tabei was born at the beginning of World War II in Miharu, Japan. When Junko was in fourth grade, she left Miharu for the first time. Her teacher Mr. Watanabe invited her class on a camping trip to Nikko National Park where they would climb Mount Nasu. The trail began at hot springs, a place where boiling water bubbled up from the earth and thick fog hung in the trees like ghosts. That night as the class camped on the mountainside, they cooked curry over a fire and swam in the hot springs.

The next morning, when they finally stood at the top of Mount Nasu, Junko was awestruck. And she realized something about herself. Her classmates might see her as small and weak, but she had climbed a mountain. And she knew she could do it again.

Climb On

Junko went to college in Tokyo and spent her free time hiking in the mountains. After college, she wanted to join a mountaineering club, but most didn't allow women as members. When Junko found one that did, the members were different from those she had known. They were rock climbers and used terms that she didn't understand, like *carabiner* and *belay*. Junko joined the club and confronted bigger and bigger mountains throughout Japan.

In Japan at that time, it was unusual for women to have hobbies outside their home and family. So, as Junko grew older, she faced pressure to give up climbing and get married instead. But Junko found a way to do both. In 1965, she married another climber named Masanobu Tabei, and together they devoted their lives to their hobby.

In 1969, Junko joined an all-women's mountaineering club that had an ambitious goal: to send a women-only team to climb Annapurna, a mountain in the Himalayas. It was the first team of its kind in Japan. The expedition took more than three months. On May 19, 1970, Junko and two teammates made it to the summit!

Next the club set its sights on Mount Everest, the tallest mountain in the world, at 29,029 feet. No woman had ever made it to the top. People believed that women couldn't climb higher than 26,000 feet. They said women's lungs couldn't handle the low oxygen and their muscles weren't strong enough.

Climbing Mount Everest was dangerous, and the expedition was time-consuming and cost more than a year's salary. Junko's team would be away from home for five months or more. Even after all this sacrifice, there was no guarantee they would reach the summit—or make it back alive.

While training, Junko gave birth to her first child, a daughter named Noriko. Some teammates doubted Junko's ability to train, serve as the assistant leader, and be a mother. But not her husband. When Junko left for the expedition three years later, Masanobu said: "Focus only on yourself and your team; complete your mission from your heart without regret."

Top of the World

Two months into the Mount Everest climb, disaster struck. One night while the team slept, an avalanche roared down the mountain. It buried their tents and trapped climbers under deep snow. The team's Sherpa guides were unharmed and rescued their teammates. It took four people to pull Junko out of the hard-packed snow. Amazingly, everyone survived.

Junko was so sore she could hardly move. It took days for the climbers' injuries to heal and to dig their supplies out of the snow. The leader made the difficult choice to take her team back down the mountain. But she told Junko and Ang Tersing, a Sherpa guide, to press on to the summit. On May 16, 1975, they made it. Junko became the first woman to reach the summit of Mount Everest!

Junko returned home a hero—and she didn't stop there. In 1992, she became the first woman to climb all Seven Summits, the highest peaks on each continent. Eventually she climbed the highest mountains in 76 countries. Years after her Everest expedition, Junko invited Mr. Watanabe on a helicopter ride to see Mount Everest. "I had come full circle as a mountaineer, from beginner to beyond," Junko wrote, "and it all started with my grade-school teacher, a person willing to share his passion for adventure with me."

A Voice for the Mountains

While trekking down Mount Everest in 1975, Junko noticed abandoned tents, empty oxygen canisters, and discarded gear. Climbers thought nothing of leaving these items on the mountain, even though it was littering. As the number of Mount Everest climbers grew, so did the amount of trash. Junko was only the thirty-eighth person to reach the mountain's summit, but by the 1990s, nearly forty people were reaching the summit every day of the climbing season. When Junko realized the climbers' trash was hurting the mountain's habitat, she took action. At 61 years old, she went back to school to study environmental science.

She used her influence to promote a new policy for climbers—"Carry down what you carry up."

Junko's love of the mountains lasted the rest of her life. Before she died in 2016, she made a final request of her son: "Let as many people as possible know the wonder of Mother Nature."

THE HIMALAYAS

H ome to the world's largest peaks, the **HIMALAYAS** are an ancient mountain range in Asia. Mount Everest gets a lot of attention as the world's tallest mountain, but it has plenty of impressive neighbors. Fifty Himalayan peaks rise more than 23,000 feet above sea level—that's more than four miles into the sky! At such a high altitude, the mountaintops are covered with snow year-round, which is how the range got its name: *Himā-laya* is a Sanskrit word that means "abode of snow." With climate change, however, that is drastically changing. Warming global temperatures are causing ancient glaciers to rapidly melt, and scientists are studying how such changes will affect the people and wildlife who depend on this region.

Today, the Himalayas are best known for capturing the imaginations of climbers. Each year, nearly a thousand people swarm to Nepal to climb Mount Everest, and more than 150,000 tourists visit the nearby national park. Yet these incredible mountains are so much more than a playground for adventurers.

The massive Himalayan range extends 1,500 miles through five countries: Nepal, Bhutan, China, Pakistan, and India. The mountains shelter animals like the elusive snow leopard, the Bengal tiger, the Himalayan marmot, the Alpine crane, and even a rare species of rhinoceros. And though the mountains are best known for their fierce weather and snowbound summits, many trees and plants thrive there: tropical rhododendrons, oak trees, bamboo forests, and Nepal autumn poppies with bright yellow blooms.

Humans depend on the Himalayas. More than 240 million people live in this region, many in isolated communities. One group that has lived in these mountains for centuries is the Sherpa people. Sherpas are known for their role as

Everest

Lhotse

Nuptse

Ama Dablam

Kangtega

mountaineering guides. This is why "Sherpa" is often misused as a slang word for guide. But it's important to recognize that Sherpa refers to an ethnic group and belongs to a particular culture.

In Sherpa culture, the mountains have always been sacred places, the homes of the gods. The Sherpa name for Mount Everest is Chomolungma, which means "the Mother of the World." Sherpa people didn't climb to the summits of their mountain home until international climbers arrived in the twentieth century. Once Sherpas joined expeditions, they showed incredible skill, mountaineering wisdom, and physical ability. The top Everest climbing records—for speed and number of summits—are held by Sherpa climbers.

Not all people and wildlife who depend on the Himalayas live in them. High in these mountains is the birthplace of three of the world's great waterways. The Ganges, Indus, and Brahmaputra Rivers begin there as small streams that swell to become surging rivers as they flow through the world's most populated countries. By the time they spill into the sea, they have provided water for billions of people, animals, and plants along the way. What happens in these mountains—the good and the bad—affects communities and places far beyond their borders.

There are three ways mountains are formed. **FOLD MOUNTAINS**—like the Himalayas—were formed when two pieces of the Earth's crust (called tectonic plates) collided. **FAULT MOUNTAINS**, such as the Sierra Nevada, form when forces below the Earth's surface push one tectonic plate above another along their fault line. And **VOLCANIC MOUNTAINS** are formed by—volcanoes! When a volcano erupts, molten rock bursts through the Earth's crust, then cools into solid rock again. When this happens again and again over a long period, mountains are formed, such as Mount St. Helens and Mount Fuji.

PLAN AN EXPEDITION

E ven if you don't live near the great Himalayas, you might still have mountains near you. Look at a map and find the mountain range that's nearest to where you live. Once you've found it, answer these questions:

- What is the name of the mountain range?

- Where does the name come from? What does it mean?

- How many miles long is the mountain range?

- What is the name of the tallest mountain?

- What are the names of the rivers that begin in these mountains? Can you trace the rivers to see where they begin and end?

- Is this mountain range close enough for you to visit someday?

Hike Like a Mountaineer

Mountains or no mountains, you can still think (and hike!) like a mountaineer when you're outside. Here's how:

1. **Choose your adventure.** Ask a parent or guardian to hike with you. Look at a map together to find a trail or path near your home. (It's fine if it's in the city!) Mountaineers always spend time planning their trip before setting out. That includes looking at maps and estimating how long the hike will take.

2. **Take a pack.** Backpackers use special extra-large packs that are made for hiking long distances. Smaller packs called daypacks can be used use for short hikes. A school backpack or sports bag with shoulder straps will also work. For a short hike, it's a good idea to carry these items in your pack: water, a snack, sunscreen, and mosquito spray.

3. **Record what you see.** Bring a camera to take photos of plants and wildlife, or carry a small notebook to make lists of the things you see.

ENVIRONMENTAL SUCCESS

MYSTERY IN THE MOUNTAINS

The stories were unsettling: tales of a half-man/half-animal that stalked the shadowy jungles in the mountains of Africa. And there were more than just stories—huge bones and skulls were also found. In the 1840s, naturalist Jeffries Wyman and physician Dr. Thomas Savage studied the bones and realized that the mysterious creature was not a monster, but something much more familiar: an ape. They gave the creature its first scientific name: **GORILLA**.

For the next century, gorillas had a fearsome reputation as dangerous beasts. But as more people studied gorillas, they realized these descriptions were wrong. Gorillas are incredibly large and strong, but most of the time they're quiet and gentle. They live in family groups and build nests on the forest floor to sleep in. They're curious and smart. They play. And despite having giant fang-like teeth, gorillas are vegetarians.

There are two species and five subspecies of gorillas in Africa, and all of them are endangered. Many have been killed by poachers, disease, and wars. Others have died because their forest homes were destroyed to grow crops and harvest products like palm oil.

Yet the story of gorillas offers hope. Because of an intense conservation effort to protect them and the places they live, one species is finally showing signs of recovery: mountain gorillas. These gorillas live mainly in the forest-covered Virunga Mountains in Rwanda, Uganda, and the Democratic Republic of Congo. In 1967, a primatologist named Dian Fossey set up the first research station to study them. When she arrived, there were only 240 mountain gorillas left in the wild. Dr. Fossey predicted that mountain gorillas would be extinct within just a few decades.

Conservationists and researchers set out to prevent that from happening. Dr. Fossey led anti-poaching patrols and joined with law enforcement to punish poachers. In the decades that followed, the governments of Uganda, Rwanda, and the Democratic Republic of Congo cooperated to protect the habitat and hired armed guards to patrol the national park. By involving local communities and introducing limited tourism, people began to understand the value of protecting the gorillas.

In 2018, after decades of intense (and dangerous) conservation work, the International Gorilla Conservation Programme announced that the population of mountain gorillas was slowly increasing, reaching nearly 1,000. It's been called "a fragile success" because there is still much more conservation work to be done. But for the first time in half a century, there is real hope for the mountain gorilla, and their story is a model for protecting similar endangered species throughout the world.

MAKE A HIKING STICK

Mountaineers and long-distance hikers often use trekking poles to help them cross rough terrain. These thin metal poles are especially helpful when walking down steep hills or over rocky ground. If you don't have trekking poles, a hiking stick will also work. It's easy to make one. The next time you're outside near trees, search the ground for a sturdy stick that can support your weight. (If you can't find one, you can also use a broom handle or similar item.)

Supplies

Wooden stick

Pocketknife

Sandpaper (coarse grit and a finer grit)

Masking tape

Nontoxic craft paint

Paintbrush

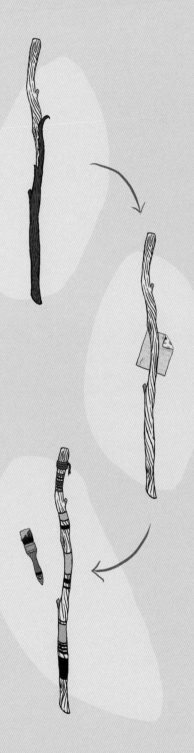

Instructions

1. For the hiking stick to be helpful, it needs to be the correct height. When you stand with your arm at your side, the stick should be about 6 inches taller than your elbow. If it's too tall, ask an adult to shorten it with a saw. (If you're not using a stick you found outdoors, skip to step 4.)

2. Remove the bark. Sometimes bark can be peeled away by hand. If not, ask an adult to peel the bark with a pocketknife.

3. Use coarse sandpaper to sand the entire surface. Then use the finer grit sandpaper and sand it again. It may take a while to make the wood smooth.

4. Now it's time to personalize your stick using craft paint. To make stripes, wrap masking tape around the stick, then paint the exposed parts. Once the paint is dry, remove the tape. You can also wrap part of the stick with paracord or other type of cord. Secure the ends with glue. Once the glue and paint are dry, your hiking stick is ready to use!

THE NATURE ADVOCATE
BOB COOMBER

BORN 1955

"The draw to me is to be out in nature, and whether you go 20 miles or a hundred yards, you can have the same experience. And that's why I keep pushing to get to the kind of places that I go."

—Bob Coomber

He left home when it was still dark. While the moon was a silver crescent outside his window, Bob laced his hiking boats and double-checked his pack. He had been training for this day. For months, he'd lifted weights, racked up miles on difficult trails, and plotted his route. Now his friends were waiting at the White Mountain trailhead. Bob imagined the view from the top of the 14,000-foot peak. He had been on mountaintops before, but this hike would be different. This time, Bob would climb the mountain using a wheelchair.

A Born Naturalist

From the very beginning, Bob Coomber was an adventurer. He was born in 1955 in Piedmont, California. Bob spent nearly every weekend at one of Piedmont's many public parks. He splashed through creeks, looking for lizards. He had picnics with his family under the redwood trees. And he hiked and camped in the mountains.

After Bob graduated from high school, he trained to be a police officer. When he started his new career, he noticed strange symptoms. He lost weight and felt tired all the time. It didn't take long for doctors to diagnosis the issue: Bob had Type 1 diabetes. Diabetes is a condition in which a person's body doesn't produce insulin, a type of sugar that blood needs to do its job. Bob's medical needs soon made it difficult for him to be active outdoors. He had to quit his job as a police officer, too.

Sometimes, diabetes can lead to other health issues, and that's what happened to Bob. One day, years after being diagnosed, Bob was on a hike. Suddenly, without warning, his leg broke. The diabetes had caused some of Bob's bones to become weak and brittle. Over the next couple years, bones in his legs and feet continued to break and he had to stop hiking. When Bob's doctor suggested he start using a wheelchair, Bob saw it as an opportunity. He began thinking about how the wheelchair could help him get back into nature.

Forging a Trail

Bob found that the hardest part of using a wheelchair was that people treated him differently. They made incorrect assumptions about him. They even changed the way they spoke to him—slowly and loudly, as if using the wheelchair affected his ability to hear or understand. But Bob knew he was the same determined explorer he had always been.

As Bob learned to do daily tasks using a wheelchair, he kept thinking about being out on the trails, and it gave him hope. He decided to get as strong as possible so that he could start hiking again. But there was one problem: he had never heard of anyone hiking while using a wheelchair.

Bob's wheelchair wasn't designed for outdoor adventures. Nevertheless, he wanted to see what the chair could do. He chose a steep hill at a nearby park as his goal and started training. He lifted weights and pulled a weighted sled across the floor to strengthen his upper body. The tough workouts made him strong. But more than that, they showed him what he was capable of. He knew that he could reach not only the top of a hill, but the summit of a mountain.

Bob soon returned to the trails with his wheelchair. Sometimes, park rangers tried to stop him because they thought he would get hurt. But more often he was cheered on by the people he met. And even more important, Bob encouraged other hikers. By this time, Bob knew those hills and forests better than anyone, down to the very stones that lined the trails.

A lot of broken chairs and many mishaps later, Bob mastered the skill of hiking with a wheelchair. He now has a wheelchair that's modified for off-road use, and he uses gloves to protect his hands. He has techniques for different types of terrain. When the trail gets too rough, he lowers himself to the ground and climbs using his arms, pulling his wheelchair behind him.

In August 2007, Bob became the first person to summit a 14,000-foot mountain using a wheelchair. He reached the top of White Mountain, the third-highest peak in California. Since then, he's summited other mountains and logged countless miles on trails. His success hasn't gone unnoticed. In 2007, Bob was inducted into the California Outdoors Hall of Fame. The next year, he received the President's Council on Physical Fitness Community Leadership Award. In 2016, a filmmaker made a documentary about Bob.

Today, Bob is a motivational speaker and writer of local hiking guides—and he still gets outside as often as he can. He's an advocate for people who have disabilities, especially people who use wheelchairs. When he was a city council member, he used his experience and influence to improve access to parks in his community. But above all, Bob is an advocate for nature. He thinks everyone would be better off if they spent time in the fresh air and sunlight. "It doesn't matter how far you go," Bob says. "What matters is *that* you go."

WAYS TO CARE

YOU: Be an Eco-Friendly Hiker

Even if you never hike in the mountains, you can clean up the trails and paths where you live. The next time you go for a hike or bike ride, bring a bag and a pair of gloves. Pick up trash along your route. You might be surprised at the difference that one person can make!

LOCAL: Pick Up After Pets

Pet waste is harmful to the environment—especially dog poop. So why is wildlife poop (called *scat*) okay? Wildlife waste is part of a "closed-loop system." Wild animals eat food from their own habitats, and their waste returns to the same ecosystem. This isn't true for pets because their food doesn't come from the wild. Instead, their waste introduces harmful germs into the ecosystem.

There are no perfect solutions, but there are steps communities can take to lessen the impact. If your city has a pet waste problem, consider writing to your local government with solutions. Here are some ideas:

Start a campaign. Encourage people to pick up after their pets and throw it away in trash containers. Make posters or share messages on social media.

Choose paper bags. Paper pet waste bags are much better for the environment than plastic ones.

Consider compost. It's not safe to compost pet waste at home, but some companies turn pet waste into safe-to-use compost for crops. Is this something your town could do?

GLOBAL: Leave No Trace

The more people head outdoors, the more important it is that people respect nature. Having lots of visitors—especially at national, state, and city parks—takes a toll on nature. In the 1980s, a group of people thought about how to enjoy nature while also protecting it. They created guidelines called the Leave No Trace principles to teach people how to do just that. Think about how the outdoors could be different if everyone from mountain climbers to dog walkers used the following guidelines:

Know before you go. Plan where you'll go and what you'll need.

Choose the right path. Stay on existing trails so you don't cause erosion or harm plants and wildlife.

Trash your trash. Don't leave any trash in nature, not even fruit peels or apple cores. (Food waste like a banana peel can take up to two years to decompose!)

Leave what you find. It's fun to investigate rocks, acorns, or plants, but leave them behind for animals to eat or use.

Be careful with fire. Only build fires in fire rings and follow park rules about collecting firewood.

Respect wildlife. Watch and photograph wildlife from a distance. Don't approach, feed, or follow animals.

Be kind to other visitors. Let people enjoy the sights and sounds of nature.

-CHAPTER 2-
FORESTS

In fairytales, forests are enchanted places. Maybe their reputation comes from the shifting shadows or the tangled vines or the trees standing at attention. It might be the unfamiliar sounds that fill the air: a surprising snap or a strange song from the treetops. In real life as in fantasy, forests are full of intriguing sights. Bright-colored mushrooms that hide under leaves. Creatures that live their whole lives never touching the ground. Small metallic insects that glimmer in the light. Resilient plants that curl and stretch and seek the sky.

And of course, the trees—the great guardians of all woodland life.

➤➤➤ FOREST FACTS ➤➤➤

 1. There are **3 TRILLION TREES** on earth! That's a lot, but scientists have figured out the earth could support another 2.5 billion acres of trees without shrinking the size of cities or farms.

 2. A forest is a community in more ways than one. Trees depend on one another by sharing food and water through their roots, and young trees grow under the protection of the **"MOTHER" TREES** that first dropped them as seeds.

 3. There's a good reason the smell of a forest often makes people feel relaxed. Scientists have discovered that trees release chemicals called **PHYTONCIDES** (pronounced *FIE-ton-sides*). These essential oils are meant to discourage insects from eating a tree's leaves and bark but are good for humans. Phytoncides can lower stress and strengthen our immune systems.

 4. Trees act like lungs for the planet. They absorb air pollution and carbon dioxide and release oxygen no matter where they grow. (For example, trees in Chicago remove 18,000 tons of pollution each year from the city's air.) By absorbing carbon dioxide, trees play an important part in reducing harmful **GREENHOUSE GASES** that cause climate change—which is why it's so important that we protect the trees we have *and* plant new ones.

 5. There are **60,000** known tree species on earth. But even more species are likely waiting to be discovered.

MOTHER OF TREES
WANGARI MAATHAI

APRIL 1, 1940–SEPTEMBER 25, 2011

"When we plant trees, we plant the seeds of peace and hope."

—Wangari Maathai

A leopard slipped out of the shadows. Wangari held her breath. Her mother taught her not to fear any animal, but leopards were the fiercest creatures in the forest. The leopard didn't seem to care about the young girl and her friends, however, as they hid under the black wattle trees. Wangari knew her name meant "she who belongs to the leopard," so she wondered if the leopard saw her as one its own. Both of them felt most at home among the trees. A few minutes later, the leopard disappeared once more into the shadows.

A Forest Home

When Wangari Maathai was born in 1940, most Kikuyu people were farmers and lived nearly their entire lives outside. Back then, Kenya's highlands were lush and green. From a young age, Wangari knew her way through the forest, finding secret paths amid the ferns. Kikuyu people had deep knowledge about the natural world that was passed down from their ancestors. For instance, they protected the wild fig tree (called *mugumo*) because they knew it created the fresh spring they needed for water. And they respected Kirinyaga, the great mountain in the east, which the British renamed Mount Kenya. Kikuyu believed that if they took care of the land, it would take care of them.

Wangari was one of the few children in her community who went to school. She was a good student, and she dreamed of going to college. But Kenya had no universities at the time. In 1960, Wangari received a scholarship to an American university and left home for the first time. In the United States, Wangari studied biology and chemistry, earning a bachelor's and master's degree. She worked in a research lab and planned her life after college: She would become a professor and share her scientific knowledge with students back in Kenya.

A Changing World

Wangari couldn't wait to go home. While she had been in the United States, Kenya had won its independence after more than sixty years of British control. People hoped a new government—led by Kenyan people—would solve the country's biggest problems like poverty and inequality. But after a few years, the government became corrupt. Like the British colonists before them, the new leaders used people, land, and power for their own selfish purposes.

The vibrant, green world that Wangari loved was disappearing. Forests were cleared for even more tea, coffee, and tobacco plantations. Public parks were paved over. Rivers were murky with silt, or worse—they dried up. The government was hurting Kenya's people and land, and it broke Wangari's heart. But it also gave her the courage to act.

The Green Belt Movement

Wangari knew that trees were key pieces of the environmental puzzle. They helped create a world where people can thrive. Kenyan people needed a healthy environment, but they also needed jobs. Wangari had an idea for both. She decided to help people who were most hurt by the disappearance of the forests: women who lived in rural areas. On most Kenyan farms, women grew crops, gathered firewood, and collected water. When their nearby forests were destroyed, women had to walk miles each day to get firewood and water. It made life much more difficult.

Wangari was a university professor, but in her free time she gave tree seedlings to women farmers. She taught the women to plant and care for the trees, and she paid them for their work. Her organization became known as the Green Belt Movement and it spread throughout Kenya.

The Tree-Planting Activist

Planting trees and protecting forests was one part of the Green Belt Movement's mission. The other part was to defend the rights of people who relied on the forests and had no say in how these woodlands were used. Today we'd call this action environmental justice. Now it was time for Wangari to stand up to the corrupt government. Kenya had elected its first two presidents in fair elections, but the second president, President Daniel arap Moi, refused to leave office. It became dangerous for people to disagree with him.

Over the next twenty years, Wangari and the Green Belt Movement clashed with President Moi's government. When the government planned to build a luxury high-rise in Nairobi's biggest public park, Wangari alerted the newspapers. Then she and her fellow activists camped in the park to stop construction. Wangari was unfairly arrested many times. Sometimes, her life was in danger. But Wangari could see a better future for her country, and she was determined to create it.

One of the final confrontations between the Green Belt Movement and President Moi's government happened in a forest. Karura Forest was the only forest left in Nairobi. In 1998, Wangari discovered the government was secretly selling sections to logging companies and wealthy housing developers. But Karura was a public forest and it belonged to everyone. When the government refused to listen to Wangari, she and her fellow activists walked boldly into the construction sites again and again to plant trees. The government responded to the peaceful protesters with violence. Wangari was injured and taken to the hospital—but she still didn't give up. Karura Forest was finally saved when a new Kenyan president was elected in 2002.

Planting Peace

Though her own government saw her as a troublemaker, people respected Wangari as a courageous leader. When Kenya finally held fair elections in 2002, Wangari ran for parliament—and won! Then she became assistant minister of the environment, natural resources, and wildlife. She was known as "Mama Miti," which means "mother of trees."

In 2004, Wangari was traveling through the countryside when she got a phone call: she had won the Nobel Peace Prize! This international award is given to people who work on behalf of human rights, and Wangari was the first African woman and first environmentalist to win it. By that time, the Green Belt Movement had planted more than 30 million trees across Kenya and had become an example of sustainable development and environmental justice.

Wangari celebrated the incredible news the best way she knew how. When she stopped at a hotel to rest that afternoon, she asked for a seedling and a shovel. Then she knelt in view of Kirinyaga— the great mountain of her childhood— and planted a tree.

THE BOREAL FOREST

In the far, far north is a forest that spreads across a dozen countries: the United States, Canada, Iceland, Scotland, Norway, Sweden, Finland, Estonia, Russia, Kazakhstan, Mongolia, and Japan. It's the largest ecosystem on earth! Its name, boreal, comes from Boreas, the mythological Greek god of the north wind. It's also known by its Russian name, *taiga*.

There are more trees in the boreal forest than in all the world's rainforests combined—one-third of the world's trees grow here. Most of the trees are conifers (or evergreens), so they have needles and seed cones instead of leaves and fruit. Their thin bottlebrush shapes prevent heavy snows from breaking their branches.

The trees in the boreal forest are very old and grow very slowly. Near the Arctic Circle, the sun shines for up to 20 hours a day in the summer, but since the season is short, trees don't have much time to grow. That's why commercial logging can be so harmful to these forests. It will take centuries for these trees to grow back, if they grow back at all. Also, old trees absorb more carbon and produce more oxygen than younger trees. This means they're better at slowing climate change than newly planted trees. Unfortunately, only 12 percent of the boreal forest is currently protected from logging and other commercial activities. The countries that are home to this forest have a lot of conservation work to do.

Like the trees, the wildlife in the boreal forest have special ways of surviving in such an extreme climate. Here are a few creatures who make their home here:

The **LYNX** is a large cat with huge, furry paws that act like snowshoes as they travel through snow.

Methuselah

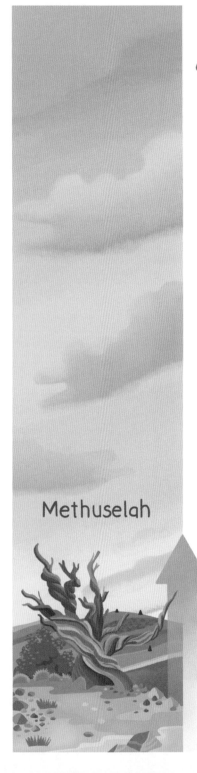

Hyperion

El Árbol del Tule

The fearless **WOLVERINE** looks like a cross between a wolf and a bear, but it's the biggest member of the weasel family. Despite the extreme cold, they never hibernate.

The **MOOSE** is one of the only animals that can eat conifer needles. Their stomachs have four chambers to break down these tough materials.

The **GREAT GRAY OWL** looks like the world's biggest owl species but it's actually only the tallest. Most of its size comes from thick layers of feathers.

The **SIBERIAN TIGER** lives mostly in eastern Russia. Because of habitat loss and poaching, there are only about 500 of these tigers left in the wild.

Champion Trees

Trees are the oldest and biggest organisms in the world. Here are some of the record holders:

METHUSELAH, a bristlecone pine in California more than 4,850 years old, was the world's oldest tree. It was beat out in 2013, when foresters found another bristlecone pine that's more than 5,000 years old.

EL ÁRBOL DEL TULE, a Montezuma cypress in Oaxaca, Mexico, has the largest trunk in the world, measuring measures 137.8 feet around!

HYPERION, a coastal redwood in California, is the world's tallest tree. It towers 379.1 feet into the sky.

MEET THE TREES

Trees cover 31 percent of the earth's surface. Some forests spread for thousands, even millions, of acres, and some forests are small, like the groves in city parks.

Do you know the species of trees that grow where you live? If not, it's time to find out! Gather these clues in order to identify them.

- When you stand back and look at the whole tree, what **SIZE** and **SHAPE** is it?

- **BARK** is the protective layer that covers a tree's trunk, branches, and stems. What color is the bark? What does it look and feel like?

- Depending on the season, a tree may have flowers, **FRUITS, SEEDS, OR CONES**.

- A tree's **LEAVES OR NEEDLES** are the biggest clues to its identity. Broadleaf trees (also called deciduous trees) have flat leaves that shed and regrow each year. Conifers have needles that stay on the tree for a long time.

SIMPLE

LOBED

COMPOUND

TWICE COMPOUND

PALMATE COMPOUND

SINGLE

CLUSTERED

SCALY

- Once you've gathered these clues, use a tree field guide or an app like LeafSnap to solve the mystery of the tree's identity.

Top Five Trees

Here are the five most common trees in the United States. Have you seen any of these tree species?

RED MAPLE *(Acer rubrum)*

WHERE IT GROWS: In swamps, fields, and forests throughout the entire eastern half of the U.S., from Minnesota to Louisiana to Florida to Maine.

LOBLOLLY PINE *(Pinus taeda)*

WHERE IT GROWS: In forests and fields in the southeastern U.S., from Texas to Florida to southern New Jersey.

BALSAM FIR *(Abies balsamea)*

WHERE IT GROWS: In the cool, moist forests of the northeastern U.S.

SWEETGUM *(Liquidambar styraciflua)*

WHERE IT GROWS: In sunny locations throughout the southern U.S.

DOUGLAS FIR *(Pseudotsuga menziesii)*

WHERE IT GROWS: On mountain slopes in the western U.S.

INDIA'S MOLAI FOREST

E very forest begins with a single tree. In 1979, a teenager named Jadav Payeng was herding his cattle along a river in India when he saw a tragic sight: snakes had died on the riverbank because they couldn't escape the sun's heat. The river island had become a desert. There were no trees or plants where the snakes could find shade.

Jadav's community, the Mising people, had been living on the Brahmaputra River for hundreds of years. When Jadav saw the snakes that day, he wanted to help. He asked his community's leaders what he could do. They gave him 25 tiny saplings and invited him to join a tree-planting project.

It was the beginning of Jadav's forest. He knelt in the sand and planted the trees. Then he came back the next day and planted more. Even after the tree-planting project ended, Jadav kept planting trees every day for the next 40 years. The wasteland where he planted his first sapling is now a forest that's bigger than New York City's Central Park! His neighbors call the forest **MOLAI**, their word for "marvelous," one of Jadav's nicknames.

Forests protect riverbanks and islands, especially along powerful rivers like the Brahmaputra. Tree roots hold soil in place during floods, and they help the land absorb rainwater by creating pockets and pathways where the water can drain through the soil. Jadav's Molai Forest is near Majuli, the largest river island in the world and home to more than 150,000 people. But the island shrinks every year because of flooding and erosion. During the monsoon season, the skies dump more than 70 inches of rain on Majuli. The Brahmaputra floods, roaring through the plains and wiping out entire villages. The river's annual floods have become much worse because of climate change and deforestation.

Without trees, floods have washed away entire sections of Majuli and other river islands. But forests like Jadav's can help prevent this destructive erosion. In 2015, the Indian government awarded Jadav the Padma Shri, a special award given to citizens who do important work on behalf of India. And in the past decade, three documentary films have been made about Jadav's conservation work, sharing his message far beyond his own community.

The Molai Forest is an example of the difference one person can make. Soon after Jadav planted his first few trees, amazing things began to happen. First, the new trees began to seed more trees on their own. Then, other plants and grasses grew. And finally, the animals came back. Birds, monkeys, snakes, and a herd of a hundred elephants now make their home in the Molai Forest. There are even a few endangered Bengal tigers that roam beneath the trees.

Today Jadav teaches other people about conservation. Meanwhile, he keeps planting trees. "My dream is to fill up Majuli island and Jorhat with forest again," Jadav says. "I will continue to plant until my last breath."

LEAF ART

Use sunlight and leaves to make forest art for your walls. First, you'll need to collect some fallen leaves outside. Then follow the instructions below to create your artwork.

Supplies

Cardboard (it should be larger than the cyanotype paper)

Cyanotype paper

Leaves

Clear plastic sheet, optional

9-by-13-inch baking pan

Instructions

1. Set up your work area in a room that doesn't have much sunlight. Place the cardboard on the floor. Place a piece of cyanotype paper on top of the cardboard.

2. Arrange leaves on the paper any way you like. If you want the leaves to stay flat, lay a sheet of clear plastic on top of them.

3. Hold the cardboard, pressed leaves, and plastic together and carry them outdoors. Set them on a flat surface in the sun and let the sunlight do its work.

4. The print is developed once the paper around the leaves turns white. If it's sunny outside, this might take just a few minutes. If it's cloudy, it could take 20 to 30 minutes. Once the print is ready, quickly remove the plastic sheet and leaves and soak the paper in a 9-by-13-inch pan filled with water or spray the paper with a hose.

5. Lay the paper in the sun to dry. The areas around the leaf outlines will darken as the print develops. If the paper is wrinkled after it dries, lay a heavy book on it for a day or two.

THE FOREST PHILOSOPHER
ALDO LEOPOLD

JANUARY 11, 1887–APRIL 21, 1948

"Like winds and sunsets, wild things were taken for granted
until progress began to do away with them."

—Aldo Leopold

W hen Aldo explored the forests and maze-like marshes along the Mississippi River in the early 1900s, he drew a map as he went along. Each landmark took shape on the page: an oak grove, a muskrat's burrow, a prairie. The teen recorded most of his outdoor adventures in notebooks. He sketched plants. He wrote checklists of birds. And he kept track of things like the weather and the date the first flowers bloomed. Aldo was learning how parts of a habitat fit together as a whole. He didn't use the word "ecosystem." Back then, no one did. But like the maps he made, Aldo would one day see the bigger picture—and help other people see it, too.

A Born Naturalist

Aldo Leopold was born in 1887 in Burlington, Iowa, a town on the Mississippi River. He grew up exploring the wide river valley. He hiked the tree-covered bluffs, canoed the river, and hunted with his dad, who taught him the names of plants and animals.

By the time Aldo was a teenager, he could identify more than 250 bird species. At sunrise, he would walk to the river bluff and scout for migrating birds with his grandmother's opera glasses. He wrote down each one—*house wren, kingfisher, evening grosbeak*. It was no wonder Aldo's classmates called him "The Naturalist."

After high school, Aldo earned a forestry degree from Yale University and got a job with the newly created U.S. Forest Service. As he rode through the Southwest on horseback, Aldo mapped the forests and watched for fires. But his job wasn't only about trees. Foresters also killed predators like wolves. They thought that getting rid of predators would result in higher populations of game—animals like deer that people hunted for food and sport.

One fall day, Aldo and a fellow forester shot a wolf. But this time as Aldo approached her, the wolf was still alive. Aldo would later say that he saw "a fierce green fire" in the wolf's eyes before she died. It made him reconsider the wolf's place—and his own—in the natural world. It was a moment he never forgot.

While in New Mexico, Aldo married Estella Bergere. Not long afterward, he became sick and nearly died; it took more than a year for him to get well. As he recovered, Aldo read books that caused him to reconsider his beliefs about nature. When he went back to work, he explored these new ideas.

In 1915, Aldo wrote the Forest Service's first *Game and Fish Handbook*. In it, he explained that certain animals affected the health of the forest and that their populations should be protected. Some North American animals were endangered because people were allowed to hunt them as much as they wanted. After the handbook was published, Aldo wrote articles, gave speeches, and started game-protection societies. His reputation led to a job at the University of Wisconsin, where he became the first professor of game management (later known as wildlife management) in the United States.

The Living Laboratory

In 1935, Aldo bought an abandoned Wisconsin farm to use as a weekend retreat. But as he drove up the muddy trail with Estella and their five children, the family was met with a surprise. Instead of a farmhouse, they saw a rundown chicken coop. Around it, all the trees had been cleared, and the sandy ground was marred with thorns. It was a dreary place.

But Aldo thought it had potential. Back at the university, he was the research director of a new project: the school had bought 500 acres of farmland to create an arboretum, a "living laboratory" where students and scientists could restore the original habitat. Aldo thought his family's farm could be a living laboratory, too. He wanted to replant prairies and forests on the worn-out soil.

First, the Leopold family turned the chicken coop into a snug cabin. They called it "The Shack." Then the outside work began. The first spring, they planted berry bushes and 2,000 trees. Over time, they planted more than 40,000 trees and thousands of wildflowers, bringing the tired parcel back to life.

As Aldo worked at the Shack, he wrote a book of essays about his family's restoration work and explained an environmental philosophy he called "the land ethic." This idea advocates for people to care about all parts of nature—from the soils to the animals—and to see nature as a community they belong to.

It took seven years to find a publisher, but *A Sand County Almanac* was finally released in 1949. Sadly, Aldo died before it appeared in print. The year before, he had a heart attack while helping neighbors put out a prairie fire. It took another twenty years for people to realize the value of Aldo's ideas. During the environmental movement of the 1970s, *A Sand County Almanac* became a best seller and has since sold more than two million copies. It's now considered one of the most important environmental books ever written. And it all began with a boy, a notebook, and a curious mind.

WAYS TO CARE

YOU: Plant a Tree

The earth needs more forests. But how do you plant a whole forest? Like Wangari Maathai, Jadav Payeng, and Aldo Leopold, you start with one tree. If you have a yard, talk to your family about where you could plant a tree. You can buy a tree that's a few years old at a garden center, or you can plant a small seedling. Some conservation organizations provide free seedlings to schools and community groups. For best results and a healthier ecosystem, plant a tree that's native to where you live.

LOCAL: Organize a Tree-Planting Event

After you plant one tree, plant more, and invite people to join you. That's what German student Felix Finkbeiner did when he was nine years old. After he wrote a school report about trees, Felix set a goal of organizing people to plant one million trees in Germany. Four years later, in 2011, Germany planted its millionth tree! Ask your school or city government if they'll host a tree-planting event. You don't need to plant a million trees—even one or two will make a difference.

GLOBAL: Prevent Deforestation

Here are two ways to help forests everywhere.

Give the gift of trees. Sponsor trees through the Arbor Day Foundation and they'll send them to places in the world (including the U.S.) that have lost trees to natural disasters like tornadoes, hurricanes, and earthquakes. Ask your class, scout troop, or sports team to join you. To learn more about the foundation's Community Tree Recovery Program, visit arborday.org.

Look for the FSC label. There are sustainable logging methods that don't hurt the overall ecosystem and provide people with jobs and timber. When your family buys wood or paper products, make sure it has the Forest Stewardship Council (FSC) label. The label indicates that the wood was harvested by companies that use sustainable methods.

-CHAPTER 3-
DESERTS

A desert might seem like a wasteland—a harsh place that's too hot, too dry, and too empty to be a home for anything. But deserts are much more than sand dunes and blazing heat. In fact, most deserts don't have sand at all but are made up of gravel or small stones. Not all deserts are hot, either. The definition of a desert is a place that loses more water to evaporation than it receives, so all deserts are dry and receive little rain (usually less than 10 inches per year).

Despite this extreme climate, deserts are places of abundant life. You just have to know how to look for it. The plants and animals that live in deserts are specialists and use remarkable methods to survive in difficult circumstances. Desert dwellers might have something to teach us.

⫸ DESERT FACTS ⫷

 **1.** Not all deserts are alike. There are four main types: **HOT AND DRY**, **SEMIARID**, **COASTAL**, and **COLD**.

 2. The hottest temperatures on earth have been recorded in deserts. The highest surface temperature was in the Lut Desert in Iran—it reached **159°F** (70°C) in 2005!

 3. The **GOBI DESERT** that stretches across China and Mongolia is one of the coldest deserts on Earth. In winter, temperatures can drop to -40°F (-40°C)—sometimes it even snows!

 4. Most of the world's deserts have no **NATIVE CACTI**. Cacti—such as the tree-like Saguaro Cactus—are native to North and South America.

 5. There are parts of the **ATACAMA DESERT** in South America where it never rains. Instead, the few plants and animals that live there get moisture from huge clouds of fog that roll in from the Pacific Ocean.

6. Some deserts erupt in spectacular bloom in years of especially high rainfall. These colorful displays include the **ATACAMA DESERT IN CHILE** that blooms every 5 to 7 years, the **COLORADO DESERT IN CALIFORNIA** and **SONORAN DESERT IN ARIZONA**, whose super bloom usually happens only once a decade, and **NAMAQUALAND IN SOUTH AFRICA**, a coastal desert that blooms with more than 4,000 plant species every August and September.

DEFENDER OF DESERTS
MINERVA HAMILTON HOYT
MARCH 27, 1866–DECEMBER 15, 1945

"This desert with its elusive beauty—of which it has been said 'its secret is secrecy'—possessed me, and I constantly wished that I might find some way to preserve its natural beauty."

—Minerva Hamilton Hoyt

In the early 1900s, people living in California went to the desert with shovels and spades. They dug up cactuses and spiky yucca shrubs. They yanked purple desert verbena from the ground. They even carried off the tall and spindly yuccas called Joshua trees. They took the desert home in pieces and planted it in their yards. Minerva could hardly blame them. She uprooted the desert when she first moved west, too. Decorating with wild desert plants was a fashionable thing to do, and people didn't think twice about the damage they caused.

Desert Gardener

Minerva Hamilton Hoyt spent her childhood and teenage years in fancy parlors and expensive boarding schools. She never hiked, camped under the stars, or even got her hands dirty. No one would expect Minerva to become a naturalist.

Minerva later married a doctor and moved to California, at the edge of the Mojave Desert. In Pasadena, she became a socialite. She hosted parties and teas, raised money for charity, and volunteered. She also discovered a love of desert plants. She became president of her city's garden club and hired people to create a lavish landscape around her home. The five-acre garden took twenty workers more than six months to create. When finished, it was full of cascading bougainvillea, sweet-scented eucalyptus, and elegant palm trees. Like many wealthy women in her city, Minerva had become a plant collector. But she'd soon transform into one of their boldest protectors.

By age 52, Minerva found herself alone. Her only son had died when he was very young, and in 1918 her husband died, too. Yet she always found comfort in the stillness and peace of the desert. Sometimes she went on camping trips in the wilderness. As she lay in her sleeping bag near a grove of ancient Joshua trees, Minerva marveled at the stars and the lonely call of the coyotes. She realized the plants she loved were part of something greater.

A Land in Trouble

In the late 1920s, Minerva visited one of her favorite valleys and was shocked by what she saw. The wild landscape had been picked clean! For centuries, the Cahuilla and Serrano people had lived here, using only what they needed to survive. But California's new settlers treated the desert like a souvenir shop. Although the local government made it illegal to transport desert plants on highways and the police tried to catch poachers, the plant-collecting problem continued. Population growth presented another threat, as California's burgeoning cities sent roads, buildings, and people deeper into the desert. Minerva knew that if the deserts weren't protected, all the plants and animals would soon be gone.

Minerva was a wealthy and influential woman with a reputation as a desert-plant expert because of her leadership in the garden club. In 1928, the California State Park Association asked for her advice about where to create future state parks. As she wrote her recommendations, Minerva realized she had a bigger vision: she wanted one million acres of the Mojave and California deserts to be a national park. It seemed like the best way to protect the land.

Protecting wilderness from development was not a new idea in the United States at this time. The first national park had been created in 1876, but not all lands were seen as worth saving. Back then, people often considered deserts to be barren, worthless places. Minerva believed that if people could only experience the desert, they would change their minds.

A Creative Solution

Since many Americans couldn't travel to the desert, Minerva decided to bring the desert to them. With her garden club's help, she designed an elaborate exhibit for a New York garden show in 1929. It took seven freight cars to carry the supplies across the country. The exhibit featured painted backdrops, animal specimens, and a huge variety of plants. Afterward, Minerva sent it to a flower show in Boston and then all the way to London! Her exhibit won awards and drew crowds of admirers, opening people's eyes to the wonders of the desert.

After her success at the garden shows, Minerva founded the International Deserts Conservation League, a group dedicated to preserving the world's deserts. In 1934, the league asked the National Park Service to consider Minerva's plan for a desert national park. Dressed in her high heels, long skirt, and elegant hat, 68-year-old Minerva took a park representative on a three-day trek through the desert. He wasn't impressed and didn't think the desert should be a national park. But Minerva wouldn't take no for an answer. Instead, she hatched a new plan.

She hired a famous landscape photographer, Stephen Willard, to take pictures of the desert. Color photography hadn't been invented, so Minerva painted the photographs by hand. Then she assembled them into two large albums and mailed them to the most influential person in the country: President Franklin Roosevelt.

Minerva's determination and creativity won out. Two years later, President Roosevelt signed a proclamation that created Joshua Tree National Monument and protected 800,000 acres of desert. Decades later, in 1994, President Bill Clinton signed the California Desert Protection Act. It took back desert land that had been sold to mining companies in 1950, created Death Valley National Park, and finally fulfilled Minerva's dream: Joshua Tree National Monument at last became a national park.

Today Joshua Tree National Park is one of the most popular parks in the United States. But its popularity has a downside, especially when visitors don't respect the environment. Over the years, trail erosion, litter, destruction of plant life, and insufficient funding from the U.S. government have hurt the park. The deserts still need people like Minerva to defend them. She helped save some of the world's most incredible habitats. Now it's our job to continue her work for future generations.

DESERTS IN BLOOM

A desert can surprise you. It may look dry and dusty, with miles of rocks and scrubby plants. Beautiful in its own way, but bleak. Then one morning the rains come, and within days or weeks, something extraordinary happens: flowers bloom. And not just a few blossoms here or there—acres and acres of brilliant orange poppies, desert bluebells, white lilies, and deep-purple clover. Together with the blooming cacti, the wildflowers bring the entire desert to life for a brief moment of delight.

Desert wildflower seeds have a lot of patience. They can spend years waiting underground for just the right moment. Some deserts bloom every spring, whereas others bloom only after experiencing a precise set of weather conditions: a drought followed by heavy rain, moderate temperatures, and no strong winds. The drought prevents invasive grasses from growing, and then the rain washes away the seeds' protective coatings, making it possible for the seeds to germinate. Without strong winds, the tiny seedlings can anchor themselves in the soil and grow.

When many desert plants and flowers bloom all at once, it's called a super bloom. For a short time, a desert that's usually dry and empty erupts in colorful flowers. The deserts of California experienced an amazing super bloom in 2019, which was so big and bright that a satellite could see it from space! People were excited for this rare event, but unfortunately their enthusiasm damaged the landscape's beauty. Traffic jams filled the desert valleys and visitors trampled the fragile flowers trying to take the perfect photo. It's good to appreciate the splendor of the desert, but we must respect it, too.

SEE STARS

To see one of the desert's greatest wonders, look up! Deserts are the best places for stargazing because they are often far from city lights and have low humidity. When the air is humid, it's full of tiny water droplets. These water droplets absorb light and can cause the night sky to look milky or foggy, making it difficult to see stars and planets. With lower humidity, the night sky looks darker and clearer.

Light pollution also gets in the way of stargazing. A century ago, no matter where they lived, most people could look up at night and see the magnificent Milky Way or dazzling constellations. Today, businesses, homes, highways, and stadiums produce too much artificial light at night. Because of this light pollution, people who live near cities often see only a dull glow that covers the sky. It's like a curtain that hides the stars.

Some people think the dark is scary, but in nature, darkness is a good thing—especially for wildlife. Important animal behaviors such as migrating or hunting depend on natural darkness. That's why it's important for habitats to be protected from light pollution. The next time you travel to a desert, try stargazing. Not headed to a desert anytime soon? You can still find ways to see the stars wherever you live. Here's how:

CHOOSE A NIGHT WITH NO MOONLIGHT. The moon shines brighter than the stars and planets, making them hard to see. Try stargazing during the new moon phase or when the moon is a thin crescent. Visit timeanddate.com or use a moon phase app (e.g., The Moon) to see when a new moon or crescent moon will occur in your area.

WAIT FOR LOW HUMIDITY. Summer is a popular stargazing time, but it can also be humid. Opt instead for a night in autumn or winter, when the air will be less humid and the skies will be clearer.

USE YOUR NIGHT VISION. Once you reach your stargazing spot, turn off all flashlights or headlamps. Our eyes have the ability to adjust to darkness, but after seeing bright light, they will take a little while to adapt. After 30 minutes, you'll probably notice that you can see a lot more.

LOOK FOR CONSTELLATIONS AND PLANETS. Once you learn to find the North Star, it's easier to see the constellations. Use a star chart like the one below, or try a stargazing app on your smartphone or tablet.

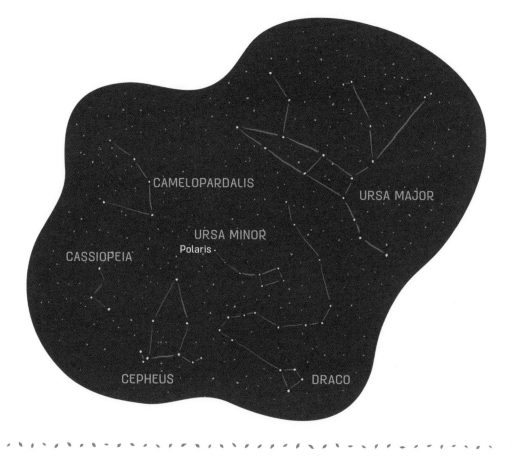

CAMELOPARDALIS

URSA MAJOR

URSA MINOR
Polaris

CASSIOPEIA

CEPHEUS

DRACO

A DESERT COMES TO LIFE

C amels are desert survival specialists. They trek across dunes under the scorching sun for a hundred miles without water, and their special hooves allow them to walk easily on shifting sand. But when domestic camels are free to roam, they eat a lot of plants and trample everything. In 1993, a massive camel farm in Dubai destroyed the fragile desert ecosystem that once thrived there. Grazing camels ate all the native plants, leaving nothing but sand dunes and rock. Not surprisingly, local wildlife—like the rare Arabian oryx—disappeared, too.

One of the leaders of the United Arab Emirates (UAE), Sheik Mohammed bin Rashid Al Maktoum, thought his country needed a national park. He had visited national parks in South Africa and saw how conservation, research, and tourism could work together for mutual benefit. The UAE is a small country (about the size of Maine) whose cities were rapidly spreading into the surrounding desert. The country's natural desert habitats and biodiversity were facing a crisis. The sheik bought the camel farm—all 87 square miles—and restoration work began.

The government hired scientists to study the land and see what needed to be done. First, the camels and grazing animals had to go. Next, people planted 6,000 native trees and shrubs, such as tamarisks and date palms. When the new plants produced seeds, the scientists used them to plant even more trees and shrubs. After the plants returned, so did the wildlife, including gazelles, hedgehogs, snakes, foxes, and lizards.

In 2003, the land officially became the UAE's first national park: Dubai Desert Conservation Reserve. Since then, more plants and animals have been reintroduced to the habitat. Here are a few:

GHAF TREE: This evergreen is the national tree of the UAE. Where most plants struggle to find water, ghaf trees have roots that can tunnel down 100 feet to reach water way below the earth's surface!

ARABIAN ORYX: The oryx is a type of antelope with long straight horns. By the 1970s, this animal was extinct in the wild; it was reintroduced in the 1980s using oryxes from zoos. Now there are more than 1,000 Arabian oryxes in the wild, including 400 that live in the reserve.

SAND CATS: About the size of domestic cats, sand cats are the only wild cat species that lives in the desert and nowhere else. They have special features that help them survive, such as a layer of fur on the bottoms of their paws to protect them from the hot sand.

COMMON SAND FISH: This is not a fish at all but a lizard that can "swim" through the sand because of its shovel-shaped head and smooth scales.

MAKE A DESERT BIOME

When Minerva Hamilton Hoyt wanted to share the wonders of the desert, she created mini deserts from natural materials. You can make a mini desert, too, using supplies from a nursery or plant store. It's best to do this project outside or on a work surface that you can get dirty.

Supplies

1 terracotta saucer

1 to 2 cups aquarium gravel*

½ cup activated charcoal

1 to 3 small cactuses or succulents

2 to 3 cups cactus potting soil*

Small items such as shells or stones for decoration

*NOTE: The amount of soil and gravel will depend on the saucer's size.

Instructions

1. In the bottom of the saucer, spread a thin layer of aquarium gravel. Then sprinkle the activated charcoal evenly across the gravel.

2. Remove the cactuses and succulents from their containers. Set each plant on top of the gravel, placing them in the arrangement you wish.

3. Scoop the cactus potting soil into the saucer around the plants so the saucer is filled and the roots are covered. Gently press the soil with your hands.

4. Spread the rest of the aquarium gravel on top of the potting soil so all the soil is covered. Finish your desert biome by adding decorations such as shells, stones, or small figurines.

Caring for your desert biome

Put your mini desert in a place where it will receive sunlight. (Near a window is a good spot.) It will need to be watered about once a month when the soil gets dry. To see if the plants needs water, try this trick: Brush aside some of the gravel, then stick a pencil into the soil and pull it out. If some soil has stuck to it, no need to water. If it's clean, it's watering time.

THE CREATIVE CONSERVATIONIST
ANSEL ADAMS

FEBRUARY 20, 1902–APRIL 22, 1984

"Wherever one goes in the Southwest one encounters
magic, strength, and beauty."

—Ansel Adams

T he young boy couldn't sit still. His classmates dutifully worked on their assignments, but Ansel tapped his feet and looked toward the window. He thought about the creek that flowed near his family's house, the fog banks that rolled across San Francisco Bay like smoke. He wanted to explore the beach as a wild seagull would. Ansel didn't fit in at school or in many other places. But when he was outdoors, he felt like he belonged.

Ansel Adams would one day become the most famous landscape photographer of the twentieth century and an outspoken environmentalist. But as a boy, he was a struggling student who dreamed of becoming a professional musician. When he was fourteen years old, he began a new hobby that changed his life: nature photography.

It was a hot June day in 1916, and Ansel's family left San Francisco for a vacation in Yosemite National Park. Ansel had never been on an adventure quite like this. They took an open-air bus tour through rugged valleys where he saw his first waterfall. He slept in a tent and built a campfire for the first time. On the second morning, Ansel's parents surprised him with a gift: his own camera. He spent the rest of the trip taking as many photos as he could.

Ansel returned to Yosemite every summer after that. He joined the Sierra Club—a conservation and mountaineering club—and worked as the seasonal caretaker at their Yosemite headquarters. When Ansel wasn't working, he explored the wild landscape and photographed its features. Eventually some of Ansel's photos were published in the Sierra Club's newsletter, and he became the official photographer for the club's annual backpacking trip.

In 1926, Ansel showed his Yosemite photos to a man named Albert Bender, a wealthy man who loved art. And although photography wasn't yet considered real art, he liked Ansel's photos. He paid to print portfolios of the pictures that he could sell. Soon after, Albert introduced Ansel to the landscape that became one of his favorite places in the world: the deserts of the American Southwest.

A New Focus

In 1927, Ansel, his new wife Virginia, and Albert took a 1,200-mile road trip to New Mexico, arriving amid a dust storm. When the skies cleared the next morning, Ansel was amazed at the desert's beauty. The bright desert sun made everything sharp and clear. Ansel met artists and writers who lived in the Southwest, and his time with them convinced him to choose a career in photography instead of music. Yet photography was still new—there was no path to follow. What exactly was a landscape photographer? How would he earn a living? He would have to find out.

Ansel became interested in a new style of picture taking called straight photography. The most popular photography style was called pictorialism, in which photographers used lighting and printing techniques to make a photo look more like a painting (similar to how we use filters to edit photos). But Ansel wanted his photographs to look like photographs, not like paintings. He thought photography could be an art form all its own, so he decided to create the most true-to-life photos possible. He wrote many articles about technique for popular photography magazines and became well known for his expertise.

In the early 1900s, most people thought photography's purpose was to document people and events. So when Ansel's photos hung in a gallery for the first time in the 1930s, the public was confused. The images featured rocks and trees and mountains. Where were the people? Ansel's photographer friends were photojournalists. They took photos of current events like the Great Depression or the Dust Bowl. Compared to their photos, Ansel's nature photography seemed trivial. But it *was* important—it just took a while for people to realize it.

Saving the Wilderness

Over the next few decades, Ansel worked as a photographer and environmentalist. Although he wanted to create fine-art photography, he often took commercial photos for paying clients, including the National Park Service. These projects gave him the opportunity to capture and share the wilderness places he loved. In 1941, the U.S. Department of the Interior hired Ansel to photograph national parks and public lands for a mural project. He traveled the country, visiting parks such as Yellowstone and Grand Teton.

Ansel believed that nature should be protected for future generations. His own life had changed for the better because of trips to Yosemite Valley and the deserts of the American Southwest. He devoted his life to conservation, serving as the director of the Sierra Club for 37 years, supporting the Wilderness Act, and writing thousands of letters to politicians about environmental issues.

But Ansel's greatest contribution to conservation was his art. His photographs of America's wild places have become some of the best known—and most powerful—images in the country's history. Through them, people can see the landscapes as Ansel did—not just valleys or rocks or trees, but something more. "I believe the world is incomprehensibly beautiful," Ansel wrote, "an endless prospect of magic and wonder."

WAYS TO CARE

YOU: Conserve Water

Desert-dwelling plants and animals are experts at conserving water—and people can be, too. Here are some ways to start.

Take shorter showers. The average person takes an 8-minute shower, which uses 20 gallons of water. Shorten your shower to 4 minutes and you could save 10 gallons of water each time!

Turn off the tap. Turn off the water while you brush your teeth, wash your hands, or soap up in the shower.

Use recycled paper and paper products. It can take more than 3 gallons of water to produce a single sheet of new paper. Recycled paper uses about half that amount.

LOCAL: Protect Public Lands

In the United States, many deserts are on public lands; these protected areas are managed by the federal government and can be used by the public. But the government sometimes sells access to these lands to mining and drilling companies. One way that U.S. citizens—even kids—can protect public lands is to tell government officials to limit these activities. U.S. senators and representatives have offices in their home states. You can call their offices and explain why public lands should be protected. In your message, include your name and the city you live in, the issue you're calling about and why it matters to you, and what you'd like your representative to do.

GLOBAL: Reduce Your Carbon Footprint

A lot of the world's fossil fuels are found in deserts. But drilling for oil, gas, and coal hurts the environment, and using these fuels for energy produces carbon dioxide (CO_2)—the biggest cause of climate change. You can reduce climate change *and* help deserts by reducing your own carbon footprint. A carbon footprint is the amount of greenhouse gases that one person contributes to the environment each year. Each of us has a carbon footprint because we all do things that use energy, such as heating and cooling our homes, charging our phones and tablets, even playing video games. Here are some ways to lessen your personal impact:

Know your footprint. Go to the Environmental Protection Agency's website to calculate your family's footprint. Then set a specific goal to reduce it. (The global average is 4 tons per person. The average American's carbon footprint is 16 tons!)

Switch to clean energy. Some utility companies allow you to switch the type of energy your home uses, such as natural gas to wind or solar sources. Talk to your parent or guardian about how your family might do this.

Eat less meat. Raising livestock for food, such as pigs and cattle, produces *a lot* of carbon dioxide—more than all the world's cars combined! Decreasing the amount of meat we consume will reduce the need to raise livestock, lower CO_2 emissions, and go a long way toward shrinking your carbon footprint.

-CHAPTER 4-
POLAR LANDS

Imagine a place where the snow swirls and the ice cracks; where the entire landscape grows dim as the sun disappears for months at a time. That's what it's like in the polar lands at the top and bottom of the world: the Arctic and Antarctic. But these frozen habitats aren't always dark. During their brief summers, the Arctic and Antarctic can have 24 hours of daylight! And in this short growing season, life abounds. Lichens and mosses and wildflowers spread across the tundra. Wildlife like polar bears, seals, and whales are on the move. The Arctic and Antarctic are challenging—and extraordinary—places to live.

ARCTIC AND ANTARCTIC FACTS

 1. There are no trees north of the **ARCTIC CIRCLE** or in Antarctica because of the short growing season and extreme cold and snow.

 2. The South Pole is colder than the North Pole. That's because Antarctica's miles-thick ice sheet makes it the highest continent on earth. The South Pole is more than **9,000** feet above sea level, and the higher you go, the colder it gets!

 3. More than **4 MILLION** people live in the Arctic, including Indigenous people whose ancestors have inhabited the land for centuries.

 4. Polar lands are the best places to see nature's most magnificent light shows—the **AURORA BOREALIS** and **AURORA AUSTRALIS** (also known as the Northern Lights and Southern Lights).

 5. People didn't set foot on **ANTARCTICA** until 1895. Today it has more than 90 research stations that host groups from 42 countries. Only about 700 people spend the winter in Antarctica, but during the busy summer season, more than 5,000 people live there.

THE ARCTIC SURVIVOR
ADA BLACKJACK

MAY 10, 1898–MAY 29, 1983

"Brave? I don't know about that.
But I would never give up hope while I'm still alive."

—Ada Blackjack

The lamplight flickered and the shadows danced. Ada leaned forward so she wouldn't miss a word. Her grandmother's voice rose and fell like music as she told the familiar Iñupiat stories that had been passed down from their ancestors. Ada loved them all but her favorite was "The Lady in the Moon," a story about a young woman who goes on a perilous adventure and is forever changed.

Ancient Memories

Ada Blackjack was born in 1898 in an Iñupiat community called Spruce Creek along the Bering Strait. When she was eight years old, Ada's father died and she was sent to live with Methodist missionaries in Nome, Alaska. Memories of her culture faded. Because she lived with white settlers in the city, Ada didn't learn common Iñupiat skills. No one taught her how to build shelters, hunt, or find her way through the wilderness.

But she never forgot the stories. When Ada drifted off to sleep in Nome, her mind was filled with vivid scenes of Nanook, the powerful polar bear who could change into human form, the *wapiti* (caribou) made of stars who wandered the sky, and the Lady in the Moon.

A Secret Expedition

When Ada was twenty-three years old, she was asked to join a secret expedition. A man named Vilhjalmur Stefansson wanted to claim Wrangel Island for Great Britain, and he was sending four young men to do it for him. He didn't mind that Great Britain told him they didn't want this uninhabited Arctic island.

Like many polar expeditions, the crew needed Indigenous people to cook and sew. Sewing was a survival skill that Iñupiat people had mastered. With a sturdy needle and sinew (cord made from animal tissue), a skilled seamstress could turn animal hides into much-needed winter gear such as boots and parkas.

Ada could sew and she needed extra income. Her son, Bennett, was living in an orphanage. She cleaned houses to earn money to bring him home, but it wasn't enough. The expedition sounded foolish and dangerous, and Ada didn't want to leave her family for an entire year. But the job promised to pay more than she had ever earned. Ada agreed to go.

Life on Wrangel Island

The gray cliffs of Wrangel Island rose from the swirling sea. It had been a rough crossing for the crew, full of storms and seasickness. Icebergs as big as train engines loomed in the water, threatening to crush their ship. Besides Ada, the expedition included four men—Allan Crawford, Fred Maurer, Lorne Knight, and Milton Galle—and a gray-striped cat named Victoria. (Explorers believed cats were good luck.) The men weren't prepared for wilderness survival. None of them even knew how to shoot a gun or catch a fish.

The ship dropped the crew on a black gravel beach and they got to work, collecting specimens, taking photos, and writing notes. They also taught themselves to hunt and trap. Most of Ada's work happened indoors, where she made stew from walrus and seal meat and sewed clothing for the upcoming winter.

Vilhjalmur Stefansson had boasted that the Arctic was an easy place to live. He even wrote a popular book about it called *The Friendly Arctic*. But when the long winter began, the men saw what Ada already knew: the Arctic wasn't friendly—it was a harsh land with extreme weather. In October, the sun sank below the horizon. Temperatures plummeted far below zero, and blizzards trapped the crew in their tents. Somehow, they survived that first winter. When the snow melted in June, they watched for a rescue ship. It never came.

By January, the crew's food was almost gone. Someone needed to go for help, but a journey across the frozen Arctic Ocean was dangerous. Three of the men set off across the ice anyway. The fourth man, Lorne Knight, was sick with scurvy, and Ada was told to stay and take care of him. She now had to do the work of five people. Besides cooking and sewing, Ada chopped and hauled wood, tended the fire, melted snow for drinking water, repaired the shelters, walked miles each day to check and set animal traps, kept a diary, cleaned animal skins, and tried to help Lorne recover. And even though Ada had never shot a gun, she taught herself to hunt and built an Iñupiat boat called an *umiak* to use on her hunting trips.

Alone in the Wild

Despite Ada's hard work, Lorne died in early June. Ada was left alone on the island. She was scared, but whenever she started to lose hope, she'd think of her son. No matter what happened, she'd find a way to survive. Ada didn't know if a rescue ship would come that summer—or ever. If it didn't, she'd have to survive another harsh winter.

Ada spent weeks repairing her shelter, adding fresh soles to her boots, sewing a new parka, and storing meat. When wild weather kept her inside, she read the Bible that Lorne had left her, sitting next to the stove with Vic curled in her lap. Ada was grateful for the cat's company. Outside the flimsy tent, the world was empty and lonely.

One August morning when Ada looked outside, all she could see was fog. But as she boiled water for tea, she heard a strange rumbling sound. It grew louder and louder. Ada bolted out of the tent. Then she saw a ghostly sight coming out of the mist—a ship!

A Reluctant Hero

Ada was rescued on August 20, 1923, two years after she arrived on Wrangel Island. She was the expedition's only survivor. (The three men who went for help were never heard from again.) Ada was celebrated as a hero, but she mostly refused to talk about her time on the island. She wanted to put the terrible experience behind her and live a normal life with her son.

Ada gave only two interviews. Her diary was eventually published, but she never earned a penny from it. Her story disproved Vilhjalmur Stefansson's false claims about the Arctic and revealed his poor leadership and deceit. Although she never saw herself as a hero, Ada had done the unthinkable: she went into the Arctic wilderness as a fearful traveler, and emerged a skilled survivor.

THE ARCTIC OCEAN

The Arctic Ocean is the world's smallest and shallowest ocean, but its cold, turbulent waters are full of life, from nearly invisible plankton to whales, seals, and more than 200 species of fish! Then there are the land animals who depend on this ocean for food and habitat, including walruses, polar bears, and birds that travel to this area from all over the world to raise chicks. People depend on the Arctic Ocean for their survival and way of life, too, especially Indigenous peoples such as Iñupiat, Inuit, Saami, and Chukchi.

What happens in the Arctic matters to the whole world. The Arctic Ocean acts as the Earth's refrigerator, keeping the global temperature from rising too high. How? Every day, the Earth receives radiation from the sun. Wherever there's land or open water, this solar radiation is absorbed, making the Earth warmer. But snow and ice reflect the sun's radiation and heat, helping to cool the planet. It's a delicate balance that's been changing quickly because of human-caused greenhouse gases.

Over the past century, human activities have increasingly used fossil fuels as energy sources. When we drive our cars, charge our phones, even grow food, we release carbon dioxide and other greenhouse gases into the atmosphere. These gases trap heat and are causing the average global temperature to rise. Each year, because of these rising temperatures and changing climate, large areas of the Arctic Ocean no longer freeze. If the Arctic Ocean doesn't have regular cycles of freezing, it can no longer act as the world's refrigerator and will speed up climate change. Our collective choices affect what happens next. Humans must drastically reduce our use of fossil fuels and switch to renewable energy

sources. It's the most important thing we can do to help the Arctic Ocean—and our planet.

Antarctic Volcanoes

Warmth is not the first thing that comes to mind when people think about Antarctica—but even though 98 percent of the continent is covered with ice, there's plenty of fire and heat. That's because Antarctica has a lot of volcanoes. Until 2017, scientists thought there were 47 volcanoes in Antarctica. That year, a University of Edinburgh research team discovered another 91 volcanoes buried under more than a mile of ice!

Antarctica's most active and famous volcano is **MOUNT EREBUS**. It has been continually erupting since it was discovered. All day and night, it spews gases and flings molten rocks.

Because of Antarctica's cold climate, Mount Erebus has a unique feature. When the volcano releases hot gases through the snow, the heat carves out fantastical ice caves and chimneys called fumaroles (*FYOO-muh-rolls*). One of the volcano's most famous caves is inside the Erebus Ice Tongue—a long peninsula of ice that flows from the mountain's main glacier. Inside, it's full of caverns and tunnels. Icicles hang from the ceiling and the sunlight outside gives everything a blue glow. Fire and ice can be dangerous things, but as these ice caves show, they can also create a beautiful sight.

MAP YOUR WORLD

magine what it would be like to explore the world without a map. No GPS, no navigation apps or smartphone, not even a paper map. That's what early Arctic people and explorers did. Many people who lived in the Arctic, such as the Inuit, developed the ability to create mental maps of their environment, a process called wayfinding. When Europeans first arrived, they were amazed at indigenous peoples' ability to find their way in a place with few landmarks and ever-changing ice and snow. In fact, it's a skill that researchers still study today. The early European explorers to the Arctic didn't have this wayfinding ability or even reliable paper maps. In the 1500s, they used tools like charts and magnetic compasses and made maps as they went along.

You might not be able to travel to uncharted territory, but you can still give map-making a try while exploring your own neighborhood. Here's how:

1. **Gather your map-making supplies.** To make a rough draft of your map, all you need is a notebook and pen. Later, you'll use unlined paper, markers, and colored pencils.

2. **Draw the map's boundaries.** Decide where your map will begin and end. You can choose specific streets or landmarks.

3. **List neighborhood landmarks.** On a separate sheet of paper, list landmarks in your neighborhood. These may include a park, well-known tree, pond, important building, school, or your own house or apartment building.

4. **Explore your neighborhood and draw your map as you go.** Visit the landmarks you've listed and try to mark them in the correct places on your map. If you discover something new or interesting along the way, add that to the map, too.

5. **Make a final version.** Once you return home, use your rough draft to create a final map. Add details, illustrations, labels, and color.

THE INCREDIBLE
SHRINKING OZONE HOLE

S ometimes the most ordinary things can hurt the environment—and the most ordinary actions can help it. In the 1980s, scientists made an unsettling discovery: there was a massive hole in the Earth's ozone layer over Antarctica. This was bad news. The **OZONE** is a layer of gas that surrounds the entire Earth. It's an invisible shield, protecting us from the sun's harmful ultraviolet radiation and keeping global temperatures at a safe level for life on our planet.

It didn't take long for scientists to figure out what had caused the hole: chemicals called chlorofluorocarbons (CFCs). But there was another problem: CFCs were nearly everywhere. They were invented in the 1920s to keep refrigerators cold, but by the 1980s, CFCs were in everything from air conditioners, foam cushions, and cleaning products to hairsprays, bug sprays, and paint. Each time someone spritzed hair spray or turned on an air conditioner, harmful CFCs were released into the air. Eventually, these chemicals floated upward and collected in the atmosphere over Antarctica. This build-up created an ozone hole, an area where the ozone layer becomes very thin.

To prevent the ozone hole from growing wider, countries around the world needed to act fast and work together—and they did. In 1987, every country in the United Nations came together and signed an environmental treaty called the Montreal Protocol, in which they promised to stop making and using CFCs. The changes didn't happen overnight; scientists had to develop replacement chemicals that weren't harmful to the ozone. But over the next few years, people around the world stopped using and making products with CFCs.

Because of fast action and international cooperation, an amazing thing happened: the ozone layer began to heal. Since the early 1990s, the hole has shrunk every year. In 2019, it was the smallest it's been since it was first discovered. Scientists expect that it will be healed completely by the end of the twenty-first century. (Some things in the environment take a *long* time to heal.)

The shrinking ozone hole is an encouraging example of the good things that countries can do when they work together to solve environmental challenges. What similar crises do we face today? What if countries united to lower carbon emissions or protect the world's rainforests by using only sustainably produced palm oil? In order to deal with big problems like these, national leaders worldwide need to cooperate. The good news is, it's happened before—and it can happen again.

FROZEN TIME CAPSULES

Scientists know the Earth's climate began rapidly changing in the twentieth century—but how do they know? Some of the answers lie deep inside glaciers, and that's where paleoclimatologists look. Paleoclimatologists are scientists who study the Earth's climate history. They examine things like tree rings, corals, and ice cores drilled from glaciers near the North and South Poles. Just as layers of rock show information about past geological eras, the layers of ice and snow that make up glaciers reveal information about the Earth's climate history. When paleoclimatologists study ice cores, here are some of the things they analyze:

The chemical composition of **SNOW AND ICE**, which helps scientists figure out the age of each layer.

If an ice layer has **SOOT OR ASH**, that can mean there was a huge volcanic eruption or forest fire.

Greenhouse gases like carbon dioxide and methane get trapped in ice. These "fossilized" **BUBBLES** are small samples of the Earth's past atmosphere.

Ice can contain fossils and fossilized particles like **POLLEN OR DUST** that can reveal information about past plant life or wildfires.

Ice Cream Cores

You might not be able to drill an ice core from a glacier, but you can make a model of an ice core—and eat it, too!

Supplies

2 push-up pop molds

Vanilla ice cream (plus an optional second flavor)

Crushed chocolate sandwich cookies (for volcanic ash)

Round candy sprinkles (for carbon dioxide bubbles)

Candy sprinkles (for pollen and dust)

Directions

Fill the bottom of a push-up pop mold with one layer of vanilla ice cream, about one-half inch deep. Then fill the rest of the mold with layers of ice cream, crushed cookies, round candy sprinkles, and other candy sprinkles. Ask a friend to do the same thing using the other push-up pop mold. Place both ice cream pops in the freezer for 1 to 2 hours or until frozen solid. Before you eat your ice cream cores, take a minute to think like a paleoclimatologist and analyze each one.

THE WILDERNESS PROTECTOR
MARGARET MURIE

AUGUST 18, 1902–OCTOBER 19, 2003

"I hope the United States of America is not so rich that she can afford to let these wildernesses pass by, or so poor she cannot afford to keep them."

—Margaret Murie

The first time Margaret Murie saw real wilderness, she was dressed more for a fancy party than a trek through the tundra. Nine-year-old Mardy (as her family called her) stood at the rail of a steamship wearing a silk dress and an oversized hair bow. It was September 1911. She and her mother had left Seattle and were headed to meet Mardy's stepfather in the Alaska Territory.

It was a slow journey to their new home in Fairbanks, an isolated town with mud streets. When Mardy and her mother arrived, they moved into a log cabin without running water or electricity. It wasn't an easy place to live. The town is near the Arctic Circle, so winters were dark and snowy. In summer, swarms of mosquitoes were so thick that people wore nets over their faces.

But life in Fairbanks wasn't always difficult. During the short winter daylight, Mardy skated on the frozen river and ran errands with her dog, a husky named Major. In the summer, she picnicked with friends and picked pails of berries. Life on the edge of wilderness made Mardy resilient. It also made her into a conservationist: a protector of nature.

In 1924, Mardy was the first woman graduate of the brand-new University of Alaska. That fall, she married a wildlife biologist named Olaus Murie, and the couple set off on a 550-mile Arctic expedition to study caribou. As they worked side by side, Mardy learned to be a field assistant, taking notes and cataloging specimens.

A few years later, the Muries moved to Wyoming, where Olaus worked for the U.S. Fish and Wildlife Service and Mardy raised their three children. When Olaus retired in 1945, the Muries devoted themselves to conservation work, and their ranch became the unofficial headquarters of the Wilderness Society. The organization wanted the U.S. government to set aside wilderness areas, land that was protected from urban development, mining, and drilling for oil. There was one place the Muries especially wanted to protect: the northeastern corner of Alaska. Mardy and Olaus knew this land was special—it contained a complete Arctic ecosystem—but they needed to convince the U.S. government.

In 1956, they spent the summer studying Alaska's Sheenjek River valley with three other biologists. They made a short documentary film and wrote reports about the area's flora and fauna. This expedition was only the beginning. The Muries and other activists campaigned for the next few years to protect this part of Alaska. In 1960, the U.S. government set aside 8.6 million acres of northeastern Alaska as the Arctic National Wildlife Range.

After Olaus died in 1963, Mardy continued to devote herself to their conservation work. The Muries and other conservationists wanted the federal government to protect wilderness areas throughout the country. They called their plan the Wilderness Act, and in 1964 President Lyndon B. Johnson finally signed it into law. This legislation protected 9.1 million acres of land across thirteen states and created a system wherein future wilderness areas could be protected, too.

Mardy Murie spent the rest of her life speaking and writing about environmental issues. There were more challenges and victories to come. In 1968, oil was discovered in Alaska, and nearly every year since, people have tried to drill in this particular part of the state. But Mardy knew that drilling for oil would permanently harm this unique habitat. In 1977, when she was seventy-five years old, Mardy testified to Congress and gave a passionate speech about the importance of protecting Alaska's wild lands.

Three years later, Congress passed the Alaska National Interest Lands Conservation Act, doubling the size of the Arctic Wildlife Range and renaming it the Arctic National Wildlife Refuge. In 1998, Mardy received the Presidential Medal of Freedom for her conservation work. Yet she knew her work wasn't done. "I'm counting on the new generation coming up," Mardy said. "I have to believe in their spirit, as those who came before me believed in mine."

Voices for the Arctic

The Muries and their friends weren't the only people who devoted their lives to protecting Arctic wildlife and habitats. The land's boldest defenders have been the people who've lived in northeastern Alaska for thousands of years: the **GWICH'IN NATION**. Although the Gwich'in who live in this remote place use some modern technology, their lives depend on the land, especially the caribou. Caribou are their most important source of food, tools, and clothing.

At the northern edge of the Arctic National Wildlife Refuge is the coastal plain. The U.S. government calls it Section 1002, but the Gwich'in call it *Iizhik Gwats'an Gwandaii Goodlit*, "The Sacred Place Where Life Begins." More than 40,000 caribou calves are born there each year before migrating south to where the Gwich'in live. They know firsthand how critical these animals are to the health of the entire ecosystem—and how drilling for oil in the coastal plain would upset this fragile balance.

Ever since oil was discovered near the coastal plan in 1968, people have wanted to drill for oil there. But drilling would permanently harm this habitat by bringing in heavy machinery, pollution, noise, and the risk of devastating oil spills. For decades, the Gwich'in and others have succeeded in protecting the refuge from drilling. But in 2017, Congress passed a tax law allowing oil companies to drill in the refuge for the very first time. The Gwich'in people are not ready to give up. "We are raised to protect the area," says Bernadette Demientieff, a Gwich'in leader. "To us it's not work; it's livelihood. It's who we are."

WAYS TO CARE

YOU: Spread the Word

One way to help polar lands is to tell people about them. Give a presentation, make a poster, record a video, or write a song. Whatever you do, make sure to include not just the problems that are facing the Arctic and Antarctic, but the reasons why these places are so awesome (and worth protecting!).

LOCAL: Write to Your Local Government

One of the best ways to help polar lands is to reduce carbon emissions right where you live. As global temperatures rise, the Arctic is warming twice as fast and the amount of ice is shrinking. But some scientists have estimated that we can save about 30 square feet of Arctic ice for every ton of carbon dioxide we reduce. For ways to reduce your own carbon footprint, see page 79.

Towns and cities can act faster on environmental issues than national governments. Write a letter to your local leaders and ask what they're doing about environmental issues in your community. Here are some topics to mention:

Carbon emissions: Is the administration taking any steps to reduce its CO_2 emissions?

Local recycling programs: Does your city have them? Do they work?

Clean energy: Do public buildings in your city use clean energy? Clean energy means energy that comes from renewable sources like wind and solar rather than fossil fuels.

GLOBAL: Use Your Voice

Thirty years before Greta Thunberg, there was a twelve-year-old Canadian activist named Severn Cullis-Suzuki. Severn visited the Amazon rainforest as a child, and what she saw made her angry: the rainforest was being burned. She decided to do something about it. Severn founded the Environmental Children's Organization, which raised money to attend Brazil's U.N. Earth Summit in 1992. At the summit, Severn made history. She gave a powerful speech, calling on the delegates to take action on environmental issues, which earned her the nickname "The Girl Who Silenced the World for Five Minutes." (You can watch her speech online.) Severn went on to study evolutionary biology at Yale University and ethnoecology at the University of Victoria. In her work as a television host, author, and activist, she has never stopped speaking up for the environment and climate justice.

At the 1992 summit, the U.N. saw that it was important to involve young people in their work, and it created the United Nations Major Group for Children and Youth (UNMGCY). One way you can make a global difference for polar lands—and all habitats—is to join UNMGCY and raise your voice like Severn, Greta, and other young activists. To learn more, visit unmgcy.org.

-CHAPTER 5-
OCEAN

At the edge of every continent, two worlds meet: the solid land and the ever-changing ocean. From the shore, the ocean looks like a single blue habitat. But hidden realms lie beneath the waves: vast mountain ranges and canyons, colorful coral reefs, fields of rippling green seagrass. And of course, amazing creatures that seem more at home in legends than in real life. People have explored the ocean for thousands of years, but guess what? There's still 95 percent that has never been seen by humans.

Think of the wonders that await . . .

⇛ OCEAN FACTS ⇚

1. From space, the Earth glows like a blue jewel because more than **70%** of our planet is covered in water.

2. One massive ocean covers the entire Earth, but different parts of it have specific names: the **ARCTIC**, **ATLANTIC**, **INDIAN**, **PACIFIC**, and **SOUTHERN OCEANS**.

3. "Ocean" and "sea" are not the same thing. A **SEA** is a smaller, shallower part of the ocean, and it's often surrounded by land.

4. The average depth of the ocean is about **2.5 MILES**. The deepest part of the ocean is at the southern end of the Mariana Trench, in the western Pacific. It's called Challenger Deep and is about **36,200 FEET** deep. That's more than the height of Mount Everest!

5. The ocean affects daily life everywhere by producing weather, food, and oxygen that's sent across the world. The ocean influences the **GLOBAL CLIMATE** by storing heat and moving it around the Earth with its powerful currents.

THE SCIENTIFIC STORYTELLER
JULES VERNE

FEBRUARY 8, 1828–MARCH 24, 1905

"Anything one man can imagine, other men can make real."

—Jules Verne

T he boy couldn't wait to chase adventure on the high seas. Growing up near Nantes, a busy French port, Jules Verne was surrounded by the pounding of hammers and the shouts of shipbuilders. When he walked along the busy riverfront, he saw docks crowded with sailors and merchant ships from the Atlantic Ocean. After dropping off their cargo, the ships sailed away again to far-off lands that Jules had only seen on a map. He wanted to go, too.

According to legend, when he was eleven years old, Jules decided he could wait no longer. He went to the docks and volunteered to be a cabin boy on a ship headed for Southeast Asia. He'd see the ocean at last!

But before heading out to sea, the ship stopped at a nearby town. Jules's father was waiting on the dock. He brought his son straight home and told him that he could travel as much as he liked—in his imagination. Although this story is only a tale, it seems like something Jules would've done. Adventure and curiosity shaped his whole life. Later, when he wasn't marveling at the world's wonders, he was writing about them.

A World of Discovery

When Jules Verne was born in 1828, a new age had begun. It was the Industrial Revolution, a time when inventors created new machines that forever changed the way people worked, traveled, and lived. As he grew up, Jules saw amazing innovations come to life: steamships that crossed the Atlantic in only fifteen days rather than six weeks, trains that linked distant cities, electric lightbulbs that replaced flickering candles, and factories filled with labor-saving devices. When the Verne family stayed at their house in the countryside, Jules often visited a nearby factory just to watch the automated machines whirr and clank.

But as much as he loved mechanical things, Jules was fascinated by the natural world, too. Geography was his favorite subject, and he dreamed of travel. He started with small expeditions. As young boys, Jules and his brother Paul spent countless afternoons on the Loire River sailing a small leaky boat. By the time they were teenagers, the brothers had explored every bend and channel of the river. They wanted to join a ship's crew, but their father was against it. He wanted Jules, his elder son, to follow in his footsteps and become a lawyer. Jules reluctantly agreed.

While studying for law exams in Paris, Jules wrote plays, short stories, song lyrics, and scientific essays. Then he started work on a new kind of novel that combined an adventure story with scientific facts. He called it a scientific novel, and no one had ever published anything like it. The story was about three Englishmen who explored Africa by flying in a balloon. Jules had never been to Africa or flown in a balloon, and he wasn't a scientist, but he had a curious mind and knew how to find answers to his questions. He spent hours at the library and talked to scientific experts every chance he got.

His first novel, *Five Weeks in a Balloon*, was published in 1863 and became an international best seller. Then the publisher asked Jules to write a whole series of scientific novels on topics like geology, astronomy, and biology. The series was called Extraordinary Journeys. With the money from his books, Jules traveled to some of the places he had dreamed about. He rode a train across the Scottish Highlands, sailed through the fjords and canals of Scandinavia, and boarded a steamship to America. Jules wrote fifty-four novels in the Extraordinary Journeys series. Each book took readers to a new destination: the moon, the center of the Earth, and the North Pole. One of Jules's most popular novels took readers to the place he loved most: the ocean.

Into the Deep

In the 1800s, the ocean was still a mysterious place. People had been sailing the globe for centuries, but the world beneath the waves was unknown. Scientists were just beginning to dream up ways to explore the ocean's depths. In 1867,

Jules attended the world's fair in Paris. He saw exhibits from many different countries, but one stood out from the rest: a submarine. The *Plongeur* (a French word meaning "diver") was the first machine-powered submarine ever made. Jules spent hours studying the model of the vessel, taking notes, and sketching every detail. He had found his next adventure story.

Jules wrote most of the story on his yacht, using the sights, smells, and sounds of the sea for inspiration. In 1870, he published *Twenty Thousand Leagues Under the Sea*, the tale of a futuristic submarine called the *Nautilus*. On its epic journey, the submarine's passengers (including the secretive Captain Nemo and marine biologist Professor Pierre Aronnax) are attacked by giant squid, get trapped in polar ice, and visit the lost city of Atlantis. They explore coral reefs in diving suits and hunt for sharks in a kelp forest. At that time, no one had been to the bottom of the ocean, but Jules encouraged readers to dream about what it might be like. Even though they hadn't yet been invented, Jules wrote about things like scuba gear, tasers, and a submarine powered by electricity.

A lot of the technology that Jules described in his novels wasn't possible back then, but it would be in the future. Today's ocean researchers do things that Jules and his readers could only dream about. Scientists have mapped the ocean floor, discovered new marine animal species, and taken a submarine into the deepest parts of the ocean. And they've finally taken photos that prove the existence of the elusive giant squid as well as its much bigger relative, the colossal squid.

Jules Verne's imaginative tales were more than entertainment; they have inspired generations of scientists, explorers, inventors, and science-fiction writers. Even today, his books encourage readers to follow their curiosity and dream about what's possible on land, at sea, and among the stars.

RESILIENT CORAL REEFS

In the turquoise waters of Hawaii's **KĀNE'OHE BAY**, corals grow from the ocean floor like an otherworldly forest. Some of them branch into strange shapes, while others tremble like leaves in the currents. Corals are small invertebrate animals, but it's easy to mistake them for rocks or plants. Coral polyps (the individual parts of a coral) grow together in colonies called reefs. Although they cover less than 1 percent of the ocean floor, coral reefs provide food and shelter for 30 percent of all ocean life, including fish, sea turtles, crabs, and seabirds. That's why they're sometimes called the rainforests of the ocean.

But just like the rainforests that grow on land, the world's coral reefs are in serious trouble. In the past thirty years, half the world's coral reefs have died. Why? First, human-caused greenhouse gases have raised the ocean's temperatures and made its waters more acidic. This puts stress on corals, which are then more likely to be destroyed when faced with other threats like overfishing, pollution, and storms. In addition, most corals are unable to survive for very long in warmer, acidic water.

Until recently, scientists thought that no coral species could survive climate change, but they have discovered a bright spot in this grim story. Some species have been able to adapt to warmer, more acidic water and they quickly bounce back from bleaching. Scientists call these "super corals" or "super reefs," and one of the places they grow is Kāne'ohe Bay. The coral reefs in Kāne'ohe Bay should've died a long time ago. Starting in the 1930s, the reefs were severely damaged by commercial development, dredging, and untreated sewage that poured into the bay. But after the water pollution was stopped in the 1970s and the reefs were protected, the corals rapidly recovered. Even today, as the water has grown warmer and more acidic, these coral reefs continue to thrive.

Hawaii isn't the only place with super reefs. They've been discovered throughout the tropics, and scientists are eager to find more and protect them. Super corals release larvae into the ocean currents that can be used to repopulate areas where coral reefs have been destroyed. People are helping this process to succeed. Today, researchers grow super corals in labs and underwater nurseries, then replant the new corals in damaged reefs. Although this conservation work won't stop climate change, it may prevent corals from being completely wiped out. Fortunately, there are teams of researchers around the world who are willing to try.

Here's where you can find some of the world's super reefs:

KĀNE'OHE BAY, HAWAII

- This is the largest bay in the Hawaiian Islands. It's 8 miles long and nearly 3 miles wide.
- The bay contains all three reef types: fringing (coral that grows directly from shore), atoll (coral that grows upward from the seafloor), and barrier (coral that grows parallel to the shoreline).

ROCK ISLANDS, PALAU

- Palau is a country in the western Pacific made up of hundreds of islands. It's nearly surrounded by a barrier reef.
- The reefs in the Rock Islands have more than 380 coral species.

PHOENIX ISLANDS, KIRIBATI

- Located in the central Pacific, Kiribati has some of the world's most pristine coral reefs. In 2008, this ocean nation established the Phoenix Islands Protected Area to preserve their reefs for research and conservation.
- Kiribati's reefs are known as biodiversity hot spots—they have more than 500 species of reef fish!

KNOW your OCEAN

We're all affected by what happens in the ocean, even if we live thousands of miles from the nearest beach. Use a map to locate the ocean nearest to you, and see if you can find the answers to these questions:

- What is the name of the ocean?

- How long would it take you to travel there?

- What is the surrounding area's climate and weather?

- What creatures live there?

Visit an Underwater World

Even if you live near the ocean, it's usually hard to see what's happening underwater. One way to get an up-close look at marine life is to visit an aquarium or zoo that has underwater exhibits. The next time you visit an aquarium, try this simple scavenger hunt.

FIND FIVE OF THESE ANIMALS OR PLANTS:

- jellyfish
- shark
- crab
- stingray
- octopus
- squid
- seahorse
- clownfish
- angelfish
- seal
- kelp
- seagrass

CHOOSE ONE CREATURE TO WATCH FOR TWO MINUTES. THEN ANSWER THESE QUESTIONS:

- What species is the animal?
- What color is it?
- Does it have gills or lungs?
- How does the animal act when it meets another animal?
- Does it move slowly, quickly, or in between?
- What does the animal eat?
- Where does it live in the world?

TRY ONE OF THESE ACTIVITIES:

- Visit a touch pool.
- Watch animals at feeding time.
- Talk to an aquarium employee about what their job is like.

THE OCEAN CLEANUP

In 2011, a Dutch teenager named Boyan Slat was diving in the Mediterranean when he noticed there was more trash than fish. As he saw yet another plastic bag float by, he thought: "Why doesn't someone clean this up?" Boyan knew the Mediterranean wasn't the only body of water with a trash problem. He researched the issue for a high school project, and two years later he founded a nonprofit foundation called the **OCEAN CLEANUP**. With a team of engineers, Boyan brainstormed ways to clean up the ocean's trash. People told him it was impossible. He wasn't the first person to try to fix this problem.

One of the reasons discarded objects end up in the ocean is because trash travels. Even items that are disposed of properly can find their way into rivers and other waterways—especially plastic, because it floats. In fact, rivers carry one to two million tons of plastic into the ocean each year. The ocean's strong currents eventually sweep it into a few areas called gyres, places where the currents spin in a vortex. The trash gets pushed to the vortex's calm center and tends to stay there.

The ocean has five main garbage patches. The largest is the Great Pacific Garbage Patch. In this huge area (three times the size of France) floats 80,000 tons of plastic trash, everything from tangled fishing line and toys to shipping containers and clouds of microplastics. Boyan and the Ocean Cleanup team decided to start there.

Team members took more than five years to develop a system that could collect and filter trash from the ocean. They made mistakes and had failures, but in October 2019 the team finally succeeded. On this successful mission, the system removed large pieces of trash like plastic chairs and hardhats along with microplastics. If the Ocean Cleanup can repeat this achievement, Boyan predicts it could clean up half of the Great Pacific Garbage Patch in five years. It is also testing a new invention called the Interceptor, a giant filter that prevents trash from flowing out of rivers and into the ocean.

The Ocean Cleanup's invention could help reduce the world's trash problem, but the main way people can help is by making and using less plastic. Each year, factories produce 300 million tons of new plastic. Half of that plastic is for single-use products, and as science tells us, most of that plastic will never break down. Instead, it will likely end up in our oceans or landfills. So how do we create plastic-free products? You could say that the world needs more dreamers and inventors like the Ocean Cleanup team.

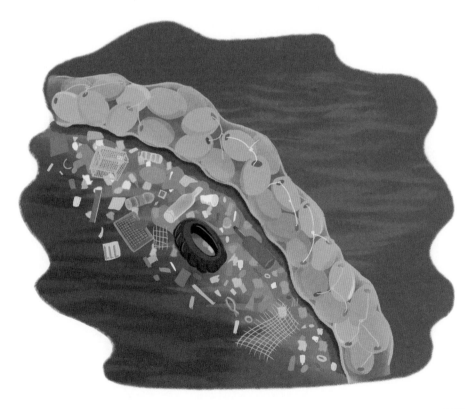

THE ART OF THE OCEAN

Throughout history, the ocean has inspired artists to write stories and poems, draw and paint, make music, take photos, create films, and more. Let it inspire you, too! First, consider this question: Which part of the ocean is most interesting to you?

CREATURES like dolphins, sea turtles, sharks and glow-in-the-dark jellyfish

WEATHER like wild storms, peaceful sunsets, and crashing waves

PEOPLE like sailors, explorers, surfers, and marine biologists

Your answer can be the theme of your art!

Next, read about artists who were inspired by the ocean, and use their art to inspire your own:

WRITE A STORY that takes place on or near the ocean.

JULES VERNE was a French writer known for his science-fiction stories, including *Twenty Thousand Leagues Under the Sea*. (Read more about him on page 108.)

PAINT OR DRAW an ocean scene.

WINSLOW HOMER was an American painter famous for his landscape paintings. He lived and worked along the Atlantic Ocean and painted scenes of fishermen, dramatic weather, and beaches.

USE RECYCLED MATERIALS to create an ocean-themed sculpture, wall hanging, or mixed-media collage.

VANESSA BARRAGÃO is a Portuguese artist who uses recycled textiles to knit and crochet large-scale wall hangings that look like coral reefs. She uses her art to create awareness about the importance of coral reefs and the human-caused dangers they face.

WRITE A POEM OR SONG about the ocean.

JOHN MASEFIELD was an English poet who often wrote about the ocean. As a young man, he trained to be a sailor on a merchant ship and later became the poet laureate of the United Kingdom. His poem "Sea Fever" is one of the best-known English-language poems about the sea.

DOCUMENT YOUR NEXT TRIP to the ocean or **MAKE A COLLAGE** of ocean-themed photos.

CRISTINA MITTERMEIER is a Mexican marine biologist and conservation photographer who travels the world to document ocean life and the effects of climate change. (Read more about her on page 122.)

THE ADVENTUROUS PHOTOGRAPHER
CRISTINA MITTERMEIER

BORN NOVEMBER 26, 1966

"I want to remind my audiences that we live in a beautiful planet. That it is very much worth fighting for."

—Cristina Mittermeier

N ature photographers visit places that most people will never see. They swim through vibrant coral reefs. They wait in long grass to watch elephants rumble past. They hike through jungles to find rare flowers and shy wildlife. As a new nature photographer, Cristina Mittermeier loved adventures like these.

But there was a part of her job she couldn't ignore. As Cristina hiked across tropical beaches and ice floes, she noticed things that made her angry and sad. She saw all the ways that humans hurt the environment: trash-filled tide pools, dying fish, and rainforests flooded by dams. Cristina decided she needed to tell those stories, too. She'd use her photography to show people that the world was a beautiful place—and that it needed our help.

Ocean Dreams

Cristina Mittermeir didn't plan to become a photographer. Growing up in the mountains of Mexico, she dreamed about adventure and helping the planet. Even though she lived far away from the ocean, she decided to become a marine biologist.

After she earned her undergraduate degree in 1989, Cristina spent a lot of time writing about ocean habitats. But it was frustrating work. Her knowledge didn't seem to be making a difference. Cristina and her colleagues spent years writing just one scientific paper, which was then published in an academic journal that only other scientists read. Cristina wanted *everyone* to know how amazing the ocean is. What could she do?

Cristina found her answer by accident. One afternoon, while she was working for an environmental nonprofit in the Amazon, she saw a man standing in the doorway of his home. His face was painted with intricate designs and he wore bright feathers in his hair. The dark rectangular space behind him was a perfect frame. Cristina borrowed a camera and took the man's photo. Later, she took more photos.

After the trip, a museum used her photos in an exhibit. When Cristina walked into the exhibition space for the first time, she was shocked. Seeing her photography on display ignited a new dream: she wanted to be a professional photographer. Cristina might not be able to connect with people's hearts through her scientific data, but she knew she could do it with her photography.

A New Kind of Photography

Being a professional nature photographer is hard work. Not only did Cristina have to master new camera skills, but she also had to learn activities like diving and climbing. She's traveled to more than one hundred countries and has taken big risks. She's been followed by polar bears, gone swimming with orcas and sharks, and rappelled into water-filled caverns. But Cristina's most memorable experiences have been spent documenting the lives of Indigenous peoples. From the tundra to the rainforest, she's learned from communities who work with nature rather than against it.

When Cristina started in this field, most nature photographers stayed silent about environmental issues. Conservation was seen as a political issue, a taboo topic. But Cristina disagreed. Seeing environmental damage with her own eyes and hearing the stories of Indigenous people showed her how much work was required to protect the world's ecosystems.

Cristina believed that nature photographers should not only bring awareness to environmental issues but also take action to address them. The type of photography she envisioned needed a name. She called it conservation photography, and in 2005 she founded the International League of Conservation Photographers (iLCP). The group's members believe that taking a beautiful photo is just the beginning of their work. After that, they must ensure the photo is seen by people who need to see it the most, whether the general public or specific government leaders. In this way, photography can be used as a tool to help protect the planet.

Storytelling and Science

For years, Cristina worked for magazines like *Time* and *National Geographic*. That is how many nature photographers earn income and find an audience for their work. But with social media, Cristina saw the opportunity to share her life's work in a new way. In 2017, one of her photos went viral, reaching more than 2.5 billion people. Cristina was glad the image received so much attention, but she knew that the number of views wasn't the most important thing. She wants her photos to cause people to take action on behalf of nature.

Today Cristina continues to explore the ocean with her camera. In 2014, she and her partner, Paul Nicklen, founded Sea Legacy, a nonprofit that uses storytelling and science to help protect the ocean by changing people's behavior and improving government policy. Sea Legacy has used its members' photography to speak out against illegal whaling in Iceland and harmful drift nets in California. It has also told stories of hope by showing how protected marine areas in Cuba and Canada can be examples for other countries. "In the end," Cristina says, "all I ever wanted to do is find a job that allows me to be out in nature and perhaps help others find the magic of the natural world."

WAYS TO CARE

YOU: Watch Your Plate

Overfishing is a worldwide problem that hurts ocean habitats. That's why it's important to buy fish that is caught or farmed in sustainable ways. Sustainable fishing means that the people who catch the fish use methods that don't harm the habitat or other species, and they limit their harvest.

You can start by researching the types of fish your family buys. Does your fish come from a country where people use sustainable fishing practices? Does the brand support sustainability? Some species are more endangered than others. Look for labels such as the Marine Stewardship Council (MSC) or Aquaculture Stewardship Council (ASC) certifications.

LOCAL: Plan a Waterways Cleanup

There's a simple way to keep trash from getting into waterways and the ocean—clean it up before it has a chance to float away! If you live near the ocean, organize a cleanup at a local beach. If you don't, host one near a river, stream, or lake.

Gather a team. Ask your sports team, scout troop, school club, or neighbors to join you for a cleanup day.

Bring trash bags. Ask people to bring their own or provide them.

Be safe. Make sure there are adults with you and never go into the water to get trash. Also, leave sharp objects, rusty metal, or chemical containers for an adult with proper safety equipment.

GLOBAL: Reduce Single-Use Plastics

Help solve the ocean's trash problem by reducing your use of plastics. Most plastic can be recycled only a few times, if at all. But materials like glass, aluminum, and paper can be recycled over and over. Here are some of the most common types of plastic waste and eco-friendly options to use instead:

Plastic shopping bags ⟶ Reusable fabric shopping bags

Disposable utensils ⟶ Reusable utensils made from metal

Plastic sandwich bags ⟶ Reusable silicone sandwich bags

Plastic straws ⟶ Silicone or aluminum straws or no straws

Plastic water bottles ⟶ Reusable metal or glass bottles

Plastic wrap ⟶ Beeswax wrap

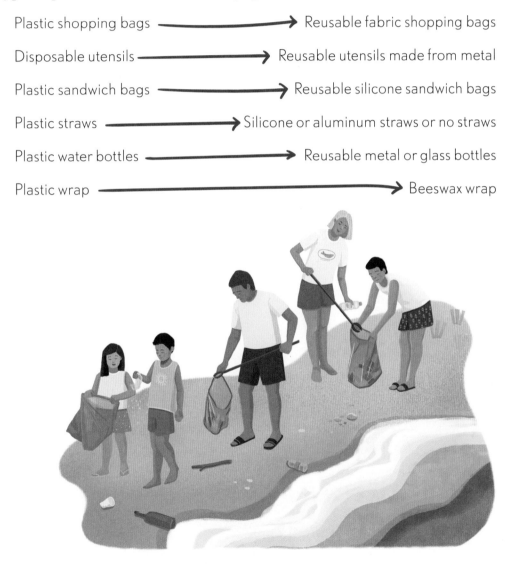

-CHAPTER 6-
FRESHWATER

We live in a world of water—more than 70 percent of the Earth is covered with it. But only 3 percent is freshwater, the type that most animals and plants need to survive. It swirls in rivers and streams, pools up in ponds, fills lakes and reservoirs, splashes down from the sky, even gushes out of faucets. Freshwater is also hidden in places we can't always see, like glaciers, mountaintop snowfields, and underground caverns.

Wherever freshwater flows, life follows.

✦ FRESHWATER FACTS ✦

 1. There are many types of freshwater habitats: **RIVERS**, **STREAMS**, **PONDS**, **LAKES**, **WETLANDS**, and places called **ESTUARIES** where freshwater and saltwater meet.

 2. More than **100,000** animal and plant species live in freshwater habitats, from cypress trees and rainbow trout to otters and pink river dolphins.

 3. The world's highest waterfall is **ANGEL FALLS** in Venezuela, which is more than a half mile high! It's such a long way to the canyon below that by the time the water reaches the bottom, it's just a giant cloud of mist.

 4. The sound of water can help people feel calmer. Scientists think it has something to do with how natural sounds cause our brains to produce an **ALPHA WAVE**, the same type of brainwave that people experience when they meditate.

 5. Plants keep freshwater clean. Aquatic plants absorb carbon dioxide and release oxygen into water, creating healthy environments for fish. Plants also absorb excess nutrients and chemicals that could hurt the habitat. **WETLANDS**, with their abundance of aquatic plants, are especially good at filtering water.

THE ENVIRONMENTAL JOURNALIST
MARJORY STONEMAN DOUGLAS

APRIL 7, 1890–MAY 14, 1998

"There must be progress, certainly. But we must ask ourselves what kind
of progress we want, and what price we want to pay for it. If, in the name of
progress, we want to destroy everything beautiful in our world, and contaminate
the air we breathe, and the water we drink, then we are in trouble."

—Marjory Stoneman Douglas

Early settlers went to Florida for cheap land, ocean breezes, and endless sunshine. But beyond the beaches was a mystifying area few people dared to explore: the Everglades. When Florida became a state in 1845, the Everglades covered 3 million acres, from Lake Okeechobee to the Florida Keys. It was a maze of murky water, dense jungles, and sawgrass that grew as tall as a person. The Seminole people lived in this region, but most outsiders—like the settlers of the 1800s and 1900s—saw it as an obstacle to overcome for the sake of progress. They thought the Everglades were useless swamps filled with dangerous reptiles and diseases. Real estate developers, and even a Florida governor, tried to drain them.

But some people knew the Everglades were special. One of their boldest advocates was a journalist named Marjory Stoneman Douglas. Her writings invited people to see the Everglades in a new way—not as a dangerous swamp that should be drained, but as a beautiful and valuable habitat to protect.

A Unique Habitat

Marjory moved to Florida in 1915, when she was twenty-five years old. With an English degree from Wellesley College, she dreamed of being a writer, and in Miami she got her chance. Her father ran the *Miami Herald*, and he hired Marjory to be the society editor. She enjoyed her work, but World War I soon interrupted her writing career. During the war, Marjory served with the American Red Cross in France. When she returned to Miami in 1920, she was promoted to assistant editor.

In her new job, Marjory wrote a daily column about topics like women's suffrage, environmental issues, and life in Miami. In the 1920s, this fast-growing city, wedged between the tropical wetlands of the Everglades and the Atlantic Ocean, needed more land. But it was impossible to build neighborhoods because there wasn't enough dry ground. People had often talked about draining the Everglades—and a few had even tried. They thought that more land would lead to more jobs and wealth. They didn't see a downside.

But a Miami landscape architect named Ernest Coe did, and he spent years campaigning for an Everglades national park that would protect the area. Inspired by his activism, Marjory used her newspaper column to drum up support for the cause, and she later joined the park creation committee. But it was difficult to get people to care about a place they couldn't see for themselves. The Everglades weren't like other wilderness areas—people couldn't easily drive there or explore them on foot. Even Marjory had seen only a sliver of this rare wilderness. Sometimes she and her friends drove to the edge of the wetlands at sunrise. They'd cook breakfast in the open air and watch flocks of white ibis. Marjory couldn't imagine Florida without this magical place. As far as she knew, it was the only habitat like it in the world.

A River of Grass

In the early 1940s, a publisher asked Marjory to write a book about the Miami River, but Marjory asked if she could write about the Everglades instead. The editor agreed. Marjory spent the next four years on her book. She studied the Everglades' history and ecology, and she interviewed local experts.

One of Marjory's most important lessons came from a hydrologist named Garald Parker. (A hydrologist is a scientist who studies the Earth's surface water and underground water.) Garald told Marjory that although the water in the Everglades looked like a still pond or lake, in fact, it had a very slow current, like a river. If roads, buildings, and dams didn't get in the way, freshwater from Lake Okeechobee flowed through the Everglades and emptied into the ocean. Along its journey, the freshwater refilled underground aquifers that Floridians used for drinking water, and it produced rain through evaporation. What some locals saw as a useless swamp was hiding a fascinating secret: this complex ecosystem provided everything from drinking water to flood control.

Marjory was eager to share this revelation with the world. In 1947, she published *The Everglades: River of Grass*, which quickly sold out in bookstores across the country. Even people who would never visit the Everglades in person became convinced the area was worth saving. One month later, Everglades National Park officially opened. But conservationists still had work to do.

Voice of the Everglades

The creation of the national park protected just 20 percent of the original Everglades, and every year this habitat faces new threats. In 1967—twenty years after Marjory's book was published—the Everglades was still in danger of being filled with roads, businesses, and homes. One day at a grocery store, Marjory ran into a local conservationist. She told the woman that she admired her activism. Instead of thanking her, the woman asked: "What are *you* doing?" Marjory was seventy-eight years old. She thought her activist days were behind her.

Marjory then spent the rest of her life speaking out for the protection of the Everglades. She founded a conservation organization and gave bold speeches to organizations and schools. She spoke out against farms that polluted Lake Okeechobee and confronted the Army Corps of Engineers for diverting water from the Everglades ecosystem. In 1998, when she was 103 years old, Marjory was awarded the Presidential Medal of Freedom for her environmental work. She is now known as "Grandmother of the Glades," the person who shared the secrets of a rare ecosystem before it was lost forever.

Lake Superior

Lake Huron

Lake Michigan

Lake Ontario

Lake Erie

THE GREAT LAKES

The Great Lakes look as wild and wide as the ocean. Sometimes they're peaceful, with sparkling water and sunny shores. Other times they roar with ferocious storms. Even the animals of the Great Lakes would be at home in the ocean: seagulls, white pelicans, and giant silvery fish that weigh more than 200 pounds. Then there are the ocean-sized stories: tales of thousands of lost ships, brave lighthouse keepers, and islands overrun with hungry black bears. Together these **FIVE LAKES**—on the border of the United States and Canada—are the largest freshwater habitat on earth. They contain 20 percent of the world's freshwater and support more than 3,500 plant and animal species!

Lake Superior

- This is the largest, deepest, and coldest of the Great Lakes.
- The lake's Isle Royale National Park is home to moose and wolves. (They walked to the island when the lake was frozen one winter!)

Lake Michigan

- This is the only Great Lake located entirely within the U.S. border.
- Its southern shore has more than 275,000 acres of sand dunes.

Lake Huron

- This lake has an underwater forest of petrified trees that are 7,000 years old!

- The worst storm in Great Lakes history—a blizzard combined with a hurricane—happened in November 1913 and was called the Freshwater Fury. The worst of the storm hit Lake Huron, where winds blew 90 m.p.h. and waves reached 35 feet high for more than 16 hours. Cities lost power and were buried under snowdrifts, and more than 19 ships sank.

Lake Erie

- This is the shallowest and warmest of the Great Lakes.
- Its water flows out through Niagara Falls.

Lake Ontario

- More than 60 people have swum across this lake. The first person to succeed was 17-year-old Marilyn Bell, in 1954.
- It is connected to the Atlantic Ocean by the 300-mile-long St. Lawrence River.

Despite their size, the Great Lakes are not indestructible. In recent decades, they have been harmed by invasive species from the ocean and rivers. (Invasive species are non-native plants or animals that damage an ecosystem.) Thirty-five million people depend on the Great Lakes for drinking water, and this supply isn't endless. That's one reason the bordering states (Minnesota, Wisconsin, Illinois, Michigan, Indiana, Ohio, Pennsylvania, and New York) signed an agreement called the Great Lakes Compact. It became federal law in 2008 and controls how the water from the Great Lakes is used. By protecting the freshwater in this region, we also protect all the lives—plant, animal, and human—that depend on it.

FIND FRESHWATER

Sometimes freshwater habitats are easy to see, and other times they're hidden. Here are some common freshwater habitats.

PONDS: Small, still areas of freshwater. To be considered a pond, the water needs to be shallow enough that sunlight can reach the bottom and underwater plants can grow.

LAKES: Areas of still water that are usually larger and deeper than ponds. Underwater plants may grow in their shallow areas, but not in the deeper parts.

CREEKS, STREAMS, AND RIVERS: Freshwater that flows across the ground is called a creek, stream, or river. Creeks are the smallest, streams are a little larger, and rivers are the largest. Creeks and streams can also be seasonal, which means they flow only at certain times of the year or after heavy rains.

SWAMPS AND MARSHES: Wetlands are areas of land that are covered with shallow water and often filled with plants. There are a few types of wetlands, but the most common are swamps (wetlands that have trees) and marshes (wetlands without trees).

RESERVOIRS: An artificial lake where freshwater is stored for human use. Reservoirs are more common in places with drier climates.

GLACIERS: A large area of ice that's been built up over many years, sometimes centuries or more. Glaciers are often found on high mountains or near the North and South Poles. One of the major effects of climate change is that ancient glaciers are melting, raising water levels worldwide and flooding coastlines.

Locate the following freshwater habitats on a map of your city or state. (Most places will have only a few of these habitats.) You might be surprised by what you discover.

PONDS

Number: _____

Names: _____

LAKES

Number: _____

Names: _____

CREEKS AND STREAMS

Number: _____

Names: _____

RIVERS

Number: _____

Names: _____

SWAMPS AND MARSHES

Number: _____

Names: _____

RESERVOIRS

Number: _____

Names: _____

GLACIERS

Number: _____

Names: _____

Choose a freshwater habitat to visit in person. Before or after your trip, answer these questions:

Where does the water in this habitat come from?

_____

Where does the water from this habitat go?

_____

Is this habitat natural or was it made by people?

_____

What plants live here?

_____

What animals live here?

_____

Is the water clean or polluted? Why do you think that is?

_____

How do people interact with this habitat?

_____

THE COMEBACK OF THE
CUYAHOGA RIVER

Imagine a river so dirty, so full of toxic chemicals that it catches fire. That's what happened to the Cuyahoga River in **CLEVELAND, OHIO**. Between 1868 and 1969, the river's oil slicks and waste caught fire thirteen times. Back then, steel mills and factories lined the riverfront. The river oozed more than flowed, and it smelled like a sewer. No one swam in it, especially not fish. When it caught fire in 1969, the news made headlines—Congress and the president finally took notice. It's hard to ignore a river on fire.

The Cuyahoga was not the country's only polluted river. By the 1960s, America's rivers and lakes were so dirty that more than two-thirds were unsafe for swimming or fishing. There were no federal laws about pollution, so industrial waste, untreated wastewater, and sewage were dumped directly into waterways. The Cuyahoga's fires made it clear: something had to be done. Pollution harmed the drinking water supply, created hazardous environments for people and wildlife, and cost the fishing industry millions of dollars.

Cleveland's mayor Carl Stokes knew the problem was too complicated for one city to solve, and his request for help was heard beyond Ohio. Three years later, the U.S. government created the Environmental Protection Agency and passed the Clean Water Act, making it illegal to dump untreated wastewater and industrial waste into rivers, lakes, wetlands, and coastal waters.

Meanwhile, some people were saying that the Cuyahoga River was "dead." Mayor Stokes and other city leaders wanted to bring it back to life. Bob Wysenski was one of the people hired by the EPA to restore the river. He often felt hopeless. "There were days when I really wondered if we were going to be able to make any progress at all," he said.

But they did. Scientists from the EPA, people from steel industries, environmental groups, and the sewage district worked together. It wasn't easy, but they slowly restored the river. Today, more than fifty years later, the Cuyahoga River is once again a healthy freshwater habitat. There are parks along its banks, and the water is full of birds and more than 70 species of fish.

America's waterways are cleaner today than in the 1960s, but pollution is still a big problem. The Clean Water Act is not perfect, but it's a starting point—it helps control pollution from cities and industry but not from agriculture, mining, and construction. There's still work to do. The Cuyahoga shows that even a dead river can be brought back to life when people, businesses, and governments are willing to pitch in and do the work.

DESIGN A RAIN GARDEN

Rain refills rivers, lakes, and underground aquifers, and it provides freshwater for plants and animals (including us!). Yet most modern cities were designed to funnel rainwater into sewers and away from the places that need it. This design prevents flooding in cities, but it creates new problems to solve.

The biggest problem is water pollution. When rainwater washes over streets and buildings, it picks up debris and chemicals that end up in our waterways. In fact, 70 percent of pollution in streams, rivers, and lakes is from storm-water runoff. But if rainwater is allowed to filter through plants and soil instead of sewers, the water is cleaned before it reenters the water cycle.

In 1990, housing developer Dick Brinker and environmental engineer Larry Coffman created a way to deal with rainwater that worked with nature rather than against it. They discovered that if they grew water-loving plants in certain parts of people's yards, that area would collect rainwater that could be absorbed and cleaned by plants and soil—preventing flooding in other areas. They called it a rain garden, and they are now common in parking lots, parks, and subdivisions. Are there any where you live?

Use the instructions on the next page to design a rain garden for your yard or school. You'll need graph paper and colored pencils, or you can use a drawing app.

1. **MAP YOUR YARD.** Create an overhead view of your house or school and draw the buildings and property lines. Then add details like trees, driveways, parking lots, and sidewalks.

2. **CHOOSE A LOCATION.** A rain garden works best when it's planted in a low spot that's downhill from roofs or driveways. It should be at least 10 feet from buildings and receive some sunlight during the day. Pick a spot on your map and draw the outline of your garden. To work best, rain gardens are usually wider than they are long.

3. **RESEARCH PLANTS.** The plants you grow will depend on your location and your climate. In general, plants that grow in prairies or b are good choices for rain gardens.

4. **MAP THE GARDEN.** Create a key for your map. Then draw where the plants will be placed. Your drawing can be detailed, or you can use shapes like circles and triangles to represent the plants. You can also add color. (For information on bringing your garden to life, turn to page 150.)

COLLECTED RAINWATER

BERM

MULCH

BERM

GARDEN SOIL

EXISTING SOIL

THE OUTDOOR LEADER
RUE MAPP

BORN OCTOBER 6, 1971

"I believe that nature is everywhere; it's just a matter of where you look."

—Rue Mapp

Rue watched the world change as her family drove away from the city. Traffic lights were replaced by pine trees, and neighborhoods became open fields. Rue clicked her ballpoint pen and wrote down everything she saw. She described all her outdoor adventures in her journal: camping with the Girl Scouts, building treehouses with her friends, and trips to her family's ranch.

Every other weekend, Rue's family left their home in Oakland, California, for their ranch in the Sierra Nevada foothills. Once there, Rue rode her bike along empty country lanes, caught frogs in the creek, and watched for shooting stars. For Rue's family, these trips were about spending time together outdoors. They grew a garden, raised pigs and cows, fished and hunted, and made jam from their fruit trees. Her parents invited friends to visit—city-dwellers who had never seen a creek or tasted an apple fresh off the tree. More than anything else, life at the ranch taught Rue that the best way to enjoy nature is with other people.

Outdoor Afro

As Rue grew up, nature was a part of her life. But in her thirties, her outdoor hobbies grew into something more. One day, a mentor asked Rue what she'd do with her life if time and money didn't matter. Rue didn't even need to think. "I'd start a website that helps reconnect African Americans to the outdoors," she said. Two weeks later, she published her first post on a blog she named *Outdoor Afro*.

Rue wrote about her love of nature and her outdoor experiences as a person of color. As she hiked, kayaked, and camped, she didn't often see other Black people. She especially didn't see Black people in outdoor magazines or advertisements. Where were the hikers, climbers, and paddlers who looked like her?

A lot of Black people read Rue's blog and wrote to her about their love of the outdoors. "I realized that we just had a representation problem," Rue says. "That we *were* connected, we *were* outside, but we didn't see ourselves in those magazines."

Outdoor Afro became a place to share those stories publicly. It also became a place to redefine what outdoor recreation can look like. Rue noticed that in media, outdoor recreation is often shown as something that must include danger and risk. But Rue says this causes people to overlook common nature experiences like fishing, backyard birdwatching, or relaxing at a park. With her blog, she wanted to celebrate those ordinary outdoor experiences, too.

Rue's readers wanted to do more than talk about the outdoors. They wanted to introduce more Black people to nature. And that's when three things Rue loved—nature, writing, and community—came together. Over the next few years, Outdoor Afro grew from a personal blog into a national nonprofit that trains outdoor leaders. In 2010, Rue was invited to an important outdoor recreation conference at the White House. Later that year, she invited a dozen people to California for her first Outdoor Afro Leadership Training. It took place just a few miles from her family's ranch.

Connecting with Nature

In the United States, Black people have not had the same opportunities as white people to enjoy the outdoors. In the past (and even now), racist attitudes and laws have made nature an unsafe and unwelcoming place for them and other people of color. In fact, some national parks and state parks were segregated until the 1950s, and across the country, generations of Black people were barred from community activities like swimming and camping. Outdoor Afro often addresses this history as a part of its trips. The leaders teach about the injustice in America's past while celebrating Black people's relationship with nature throughout history.

One relationship that Outdoor Afro works to strengthen is Black people's connection to water. "Having a relationship with water means Black people will have a greater stake in its conservation," Rue says, "as well as a skill that saves lives and is a gateway to many other outdoor activities." Outdoor Afro has a scholarship fund for swimming lessons, and local chapters host fishing trips to connect members to waterways where they live. Every year, Rue leads a whitewater rafting trip on the American River in California.

An Outdoor Community

The raft bounces as it hits the rapids, and Rue tightens her grip on the paddle. Behind her, other rafts splash through the waves. They are filled with her friends, whose shouts and laughter echo along the river. Rue couldn't have imagined this scene when she published her first blog post. Back then, she thought she was alone. Today, the community she's created stretches across the United States. Now there are more than 45,000 Outdoor Afro members who join 90 local leaders on monthly outings and conservation work.

Since her childhood on the ranch, Rue has climbed mountains, rafted rivers, joined an expedition to the Arctic, been honored by *National Geographic*, joined the Wilderness Society, and launched a movement—all because she took one step to share her love of nature with others.

WAYS TO CARE

YOU: Plant a Rain Garden

If you designed a rain garden on page 144, now is the time to plant it! First, find an adult helper. Many cities have rules about gardens, and there are *very* important safety precautions to be aware of, like avoiding underground cables or pipes. (Ask an adult to call 811 before you dig.) Once your garden is planted, just wait for the rain to fall. After a heavy downpour, most rain gardens will remain filled with water for a day or two before the water soaks into the ground.

LOCAL: Share What You Learn

Sometimes the best way to protect a habitat is to share what you learn, like Marjory Stoneman Douglas did. Is there a freshwater habitat in your community that's being overlooked or polluted? Learn about it and share your knowledge with others. Here's how:

MAKE A DOCUMENTARY. Film the habitat at different times of the day in different seasons. Include footage of the plants and animals that live there (but keep a respectful distance).

CREATE A PHOTO BOOK. Tell the story of the habitat through your own photos.

WRITE A STORY. Develop a nonfiction story or try writing fiction—for example, describing the habitat through the eyes of a creature who lives there.

GLOBAL: Drinking Water for All

Millions of people don't have clean drinking water. Sometimes they live in places where the only water is in polluted streams. Sometimes the water that pours from their faucets isn't safe to drink. It's a global problem, but there are people working on solutions such as building wells and distributing water filters to communities in need. Here are some inspiring kids who are making a difference:

MARI C. is a 13-year-old from Flint, Michigan, who brought national attention to the unsafe drinking water in her hometown. She's also organized weekly events where residents can get free drinking water.

ADDYSON M., a 10-year-old from Missouri, raised money for clean water charities by running half marathons and asking for sponsors.

NATHAN M., a third grader in Illinois, asked his class to give the money from their weekly Donut Day sale to an organization that builds wells. They raised more than $2,000—enough to build five wells!

-CHAPTER 7-
CITIES

If you live in a city, you might think of nature as a place to visit. Beyond the busy streets, without stores or traffic or people. But nature is everywhere, and a city is a habitat all its own, with plants and animals that have found ways to thrive in urban settings. Think of the vacant lot full of clover and buzzing insects. The pond in a suburban subdivision where ducks build nests. A rooftop garden. The gulls that gather in parking lots.

The question isn't whether or not nature exists in cities. The question is: Can you see it?

⌁ CITIES FACTS ⌁

 1. Cities are often known for destroying **WILDLIFE HABITAT**. But some animals can adapt if we're willing to find ways to coexist. Though they're often considered pests, these animals can thrive in cities: raccoons, pigeons, opossums, gulls, coyotes, bats, foxes—even leopards!

 2. A vacant urban lot might not be much to look at, but it can contain as many as **50 SPECIES** of plants and animals. That's a lot of biodiversity!

 3. **STREET TREES** are more than just decoration. Research shows they reduce air pollution, provide habitat, and can lower temperatures by as much as 4 degrees.

4. **BIRDS** that live in cities change their songs to be heard over the noise. Their songs are often louder and higher pitched than those of birds that don't live in cities.

 5. Public green space is areas like forests, nature preserves, parks, and gardens. In some cities more than **40%** of the land is public green space: Prague, Czech Republic; Madrid, Spain; Edinburgh, Scotland; and Auckland, New Zealand.

THE PARK ARCHITECT
FREDERICK LAW OLMSTED

APRIL 26, 1822–AUGUST 28, 1903

"Guard against the impulse to fill up space with things."

—Frederick Law Olmsted

t was a terrible place for a park. Fred kicked at the gravel-covered ground and squinted at the work crews in the distance. Nothing could grow in this soil, and all the trees were long gone. Most had been cut down during the American Revolution, and the rest chopped up and hauled away by city residents. Trash was strewn everywhere and a stench drifted out from nearby slaughterhouses.

Poor location or not, Fred had to help turn this land into New York City's first public park. Fred was a farmer, and he knew how to make good things come from soil. But by the time Central Park was completed, he wouldn't be a farmer anymore. Frederick Law Olmsted would have a new title: America's first landscape architect.

Until the 1850s, there was no such thing as public city parks in the United States. Rich people had private gardens, but most city residents had just one place to go for fresh air and nature: a cemetery. In cities like New York, people went for walks and picnicked among the headstones. Unlike most urban places, cemeteries often had areas of green grass and trees. Maybe even flowers. It was better than nothing.

The Scientific Farmer

Frederick Law Olmsted was born in 1822, when America was still a young country. Fred grew into a restless young man, full of ideas and energy that he wasn't sure how to use. He switched from one job to the next: first he was a surveyor's apprentice, then a clerk, then a sailor. When he returned from a yearlong voyage to China, Fred had another new idea: he wanted to be a scientific farmer.

In Fred's time, agriculture was a new branch of science. Scientific farmers used agricultural science and technology in their farming methods. Fred's first farm was a failure, but then his father bought him a bigger farm in a better location, where Fred successfully grew peaches, pears, corn, and cabbage. He could even afford to hire a staff.

In 1850, Fred left the farm behind and took a six-month walking tour of England. The English countryside was one of the most beautiful places he had ever seen. As Fred and two friends hiked from village to village, he loved to explore the rolling meadows and forests. Along the way, Fred visited a new kind of city park in Birkenhead, England. Other European cities had public parks, which were owned by royalty or rich aristocrats. Birkenhead Park was the first publicly funded park in the world. Not only was the park open to ordinary citizens, it was also "owned" by them.

Birkenhead Park's designers had re-created the beauty and peace of the countryside within a busy city. But it wasn't just the design that caught Fred's attention. As he strolled along the winding paths, he noticed something unusual for the time: the park was filled with many different kinds of people: men, women, and children from all social classes. The sight stayed with him long after he returned home.

A New Kind of Park

Back in the United States, Fred became a journalist. He wrote two books about his travels and worked as an undercover reporter for the brand-new newspaper the *New York Times*. He traveled through the American South reporting on all he saw and heard. The experience turned him into an abolitionist, and his newspaper columns were later used win British support for the Union during the Civil War.

In the fall of 1857, Fred was once again looking for a new career when he was hired to be the superintendent of a park project in Manhattan. A few months after getting the job, the city held a design competition for the new park. Calvert Vaux, an English architect, asked Fred to be his partner in the contest. Fred had no architecture training, but he knew how to work with land. As park superintendent, he managed huge work crews, clearing brush, blasting rocks, and digging trenches for streams and ponds. He knew the future park's terrain better than anyone.

The two men worked tirelessly on their design. They drew blueprints filled with incredible detail, including more than a thousand hand-drawn trees. They even hired an artist to paint an example of what the new park could look like. The competition had 33 entries—and Fred and Calvert's design won.

Then the real work began. It would take years to transform the 840 acres into a park. Like Birkenhead Park, Fred and Calvert's design re-created the country-side within a city setting. They planned quiet meadows, hidden groves, stone buildings, and rock outcroppings. At every spot, Fred looked at the scenery through the eyes of an artist. The worn-out land beneath his feet had become his canvas.

Places for People and Nature

Central Park was the beginning of Fred's long career as a landscape architect. The park was so popular that other U.S. cities wanted Fred and Calvert to de-sign their parks, too. Their next project was Brooklyn's Prospect Park, and then they designed the country's first park system in Buffalo, New York. Fred and Calvert worked together for many years before parting ways. One of their last projects together was Niagara Falls State Park in New York, the first state park in the United States.

Later in life, Fred moved to Connecticut and opened his own landscape archi-tecture firm with his sons. Together, they designed more than 500 landscape projects, including 100 parks, 40 college campuses, 200 private estates, and 50 subdivisions. Fred's imagination defined what a public park could be and creat-ed beautiful places across America where people could access nature—just as he had witnessed in Birkenhead Park all those years ago.

Through it all, Fred knew that he'd never see the long-term results of his work. As a landscape architect, he understood that it would take years before his parks would mature and match his original design. But he was willing to do the work anyway. Fred understood that the saplings he planted in his own time would one day grow into mighty trees.

CITIES GO GREEN

Cities have a reputation for paving over nature, pushing out animals, and creating pollution. But it doesn't have to be that way. Some cities are working hard to help nature thrive.

Copenhagen, Denmark

In just four years, Copenhagen cut its carbon emissions by 61 percent! One of the reasons is fewer cars. More than half of Copenhagen's residents bike to work. The Green Path is a 5-mile trail that takes bike commuters through some of the city's most beautiful scenery. Copenhagen is also home to Copenhill, a clean power plant that burns waste instead of fossil fuels. The futuristic building is topped by a public park with a hiking trail, climbing wall, gardens, even an artificial ski and snowboard hill!

Singapore

Singapore is both a city and a country that's packed with high-rise buildings. But as its population has grown, so has its urban nature. Whenever a new building goes up, the greenery that's lost on the ground is replaced somewhere else. One way builders do this is by incorporating rooftop gardens and vertical walls of plants in their designs. But it's not just buildings. Whenever a new road is built in Singapore, there's space set aside for tree planting. Each year, Singapore's National Park Board plants 50,000 new trees along streets and in parks.

San Francisco, California

San Francisco has a long eco-friendly history, but the city's most recent success involves a challenge that all cities face: trash. In the United States, only about 34 percent of trash is recycled or composted. In San Francisco, by contrast, 80 percent of waste is recycled or composted. It hasn't always been this way. The city created strict rules and an efficient recycling and composting program to reach this goal. In many places, food waste makes up 20 percent of landfills, but in San Francisco that waste is turned into fertilizer. Food scraps (and yard waste) are picked up each week across the city and delivered to a company that turns them into organic fertilizer.

Other Cities

Even as countries have struggled to meet their climate change goals, some cities are succeeding. Here are large cities that have reduced their carbon emissions by 20 percent or more:

- London, England
- San Francisco, California (U.S.)
- Madrid, Spain
- Toronto, Ontario (Canada)
- Berlin, Germany
- Tokyo, Japan

MAKE AN URBAN
NATURE DOCUMENTARY

Nature documentaries are often filmed in places where there aren't any people. They show amazing wildlife, but it's far away from most people's everyday lives. What about the nature that's nearby? There are plenty of places where plants, animals, and people coexist. Even in a city, nature is waiting under the rumble of traffic and along the sidewalks. One way to find it is to make an urban nature documentary.

1. **Gather your equipment.** In most cases you'll need a camera or smartphone and a video editing app.

2. **Brainstorm locations and specific things to film.**.

3. **Record your videos.** Take a walk or bike ride in your neighborhood and record videos of the nature you see. Use your brainstorm list if it helps. You might also want to narrate the video to tell viewers what they're seeing.

4. **Edit your video footage using a video editing app.** Then invent a title for your nature documentary.

5. **Have a premiere.** Share your documentary with friends and family.

Here are some things to include in your documentary:

PLANTS: Look for garden plants but also plants that people might consider to be weeds. Where's the most interesting place a plant is growing in your neighborhood?

INSECTS: Sidewalks and plants are good places to find them.

BIRDS: Keep an eye out for signs of bird activity, like feathers or nests. If you can't see any birds, try to record their songs or calls.

MAMMALS: Mammals in the city can be a bit shy, but you can still look for their tracks or homes such as burrows.

REPTILES/AMPHIBIANS: If you can't see these creatures, sometimes you can still hear them.

FISH: Fish can be hard to spot since they live underwater, but sometimes you can see them come to the surface to feed.

ENVIRONMENTAL CONCERNS: You might want to include the not-so-great things, too, like litter or polluted water. These things can show the work that needs to be done to better care for the nature in your community.

UNEARTHING SEOUL'S
HIDDEN STREAM

In the days before highways and skyscrapers, a wild stream ran through a kingdom in Asia. Over the centuries, people tamed the stream. In the 1400s, it flooded people's homes, so they turned the stream into a canal. As the kingdom grew into South Korea's capital city in the twentieth century, the **CHEONGGYECHEON STREAM** became an open sewer. Sometimes its water was blue or black. It became such an eyesore—and a health hazard—that it was covered with concrete and steel. By 1976, instead of a waterway in the center of Seoul, there was a noisy freeway.

What happened to Cheonggyecheon Stream is not unusual. Throughout history, rivers and streams have been buried to help with flooding and waste disposal. That worked in the short term, but we now know that natural waterways are better for cities. When they disappear, more than just water is lost. Gone, too, are habitats for wildlife and plants, flood control, cooler air temperatures, and peaceful places where people can be in nature.

Since the 1980s, cities worldwide have been unearthing once-covered waterways, a process called daylighting. One of the biggest projects was Cheonggyecheon Stream. In 2001, Korean urban planners led by Dr. Kee Yeon Hwang developed a plan to remove the freeway in downtown Seoul and create a park around the long-buried stream. The road was demolished, traffic was rerouted, buildings were razed, and trees were planted. Today the stream flows through a public park that's nearly four miles long and lined with trees and walking paths.

Completed in 2005, the Cheonggyecheon restoration project isn't perfect and the works continue, but the positive effects are encouraging. The stream acts as a natural air-conditioner—the surrounding air is often five degrees cooler than the rest of the city—and during heavy rainfall, it helps prevent flash floods. Replacing a freeway with a park has also reduced the neighborhood's air pollution by 35 percent.

That's not all. The stream's reappearance brought back flora and wildlife, including more than 300 plant species, 25 fish species, and 36 types of birds. People love the park, and more than 60,000 visitors pass through each day. But perhaps the biggest accomplishment of the Cheonggyecheon project is that it has inspired other cities to restore their streams and rivers. In many ways, river restoration can help urban areas deal with the effects of climate change, especially higher temperatures and increased flooding. These are some places where lost rivers have been restored:

ZURICH, SWITZERLAND

VANCOUVER, BRITISH COLUMBIA

AUCKLAND, NEW ZEALAND

SHEFFIELD, ENGLAND

LONDON, ENGLAND

YONKERS, NEW YORK (U.S.)

SEATTLE, WASHINGTON (U.S.)

KALAMAZOO, MICHIGAN (U.S.)

MAKE A BIRD FEEDER

One way to get a closer look at city songbirds is to set up a birdfeeder. Some birds will eat seeds from a feeder where they can perch. Other species—like mourning doves and sparrows—prefer to eat seeds that fall on the ground. Some birds will probably never show up at a bird feeder, like robins, who prefer insects and fruit they find on their own. Make a bird feeder from recycled materials, fill it with birdseed, and then see who shows up!

Supplies

1 metal can

Colored duct tape

Craft glue

Thin wooden dowel

18-inch piece of twine
  or craft cord

Birdseed

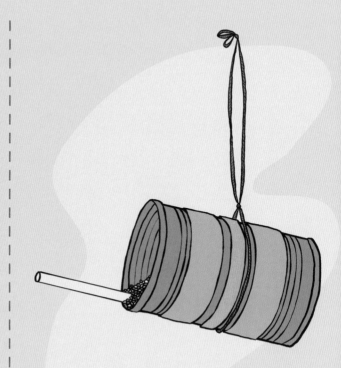

Instructions

1. Rinse and dry the can. (Be careful of sharp edges!)

2. Decorate the outside of the can with duct tape. Use two or more tape colors to make stripes or other designs.

3. Glue the wooden dowel inside the can so that at least two inches stick out. This will be the perch where birds land.

4. Tie the twine around the middle of the can and secure with a knot. Tie another knot at the ends of the twine to make a loop.

5. Fill the bird feeder with birdseed and ask an adult to help hang it.

Birdseed 101

What birds will visit your feeder? That depends on where you live and the type of seed you supply.

SUNFLOWER SEEDS = nearly all songbirds, including cardinals, chickadees, sparrows, and finches

SAFFLOWER SEEDS = chickadees, grosbeaks, finches, sparrows

THISTLE SEEDS = finches, chickadees

WHOLE PEANUTS = jays, woodpeckers

CRACKED CORN = sparrows, woodpeckers

MILLET = wrens, juncos

THE RENEGADE GARDENER
RON FINLEY

BORN 20TH CENTURY

"Gardening is the most therapeutic and defiant act you can do,
especially in the inner city."

—Ron Finley

The garden was against the law. The wavy kale leaves and spirals of pumpkin vines, the plump tomatoes and celery stalks, even the sunflowers—all of it was illegal. When Ron Finley dropped those first seeds into the dirt, he had no idea what was to come. The land between the sidewalk and the street was just a narrow strip of sun-scorched weeds. It didn't attract a single bug or bird. So when Ron and some friends planted a garden there, it was an unusual sight. People didn't really plant gardens in South Los Angeles.

But soon Ron's neighbors realized how beautiful it was—a green oasis surrounded by concrete. It was full of fresh food, which Ron gave away to residents. The garden didn't have a fence. Someone once asked Ron if he was afraid people would steal his fruits and vegetables. Ron said that was the point: to share it. The food led to conversations, and the conversations led to community. But then, in the spring of 2011, city officials told him to cut it all down.

The city had rules about parkways, the strip of land where Ron planted his garden. They issued him a citation: a fine sort of like a speeding ticket, but for growing plants instead of driving too fast. It wasn't the first time. Years earlier, Ron had planted banana trees in the same spot. The city issued him a citation then, too, and he had to chop down the trees.

But this time, Ron wouldn't cut down his garden. He was going to let it grow.

Seeds of Change

Ron had lived his whole life in South Los Angeles, and he saw things that needed to change. His city is one of many "food deserts" in the United States. A food desert is a place where people can't buy affordable healthy food like fresh vegetables because there are no stores nearby that sell them. Most of the food in Ron's neighborhood came from gas stations and fast food restaurants. There wasn't a single grocery store. When people don't have nutritious food to eat, they get sick. And many people in South Los Angeles had health problems like heart disease and asthma.

Ron was tired of seeing his neighbors struggle. And he was tired of driving forty-five minutes just to buy an organic apple. So he took a gardening class and helped create a volunteer organization called LA Green Grounds. The group's goal was to plant edible gardens all over South Los Angeles and teach people to grow their own food. They would learn about gardening and nutrition at the same time. Ron's garden was among the first ones they planted. And now it was in trouble.

Ron challenged the city's citation. The city issued a warrant for his arrest. If he didn't dig up his garden, he would go to jail. But Ron had people on his side. A newspaper reporter shared his story in the *Los Angeles Times*. A friend from LA Green Grounds started a petition and gathered 900 signatures. Then a city council member got involved. The councilor supported Ron and worked to change the rules. The garden could stay. And from then on, it was legal to plant gardens on parkways.

An Urban Oasis

A city garden is a source of fresh food, but it also creates something that's harder to measure. In a place that has more vacant lots than public parks, Ron's garden adds beauty.

Before Ron was a gardener, he was an artist and fashion designer. Now gardening is his art. "I use the soil like it's a piece of cloth, and the plants and the trees, that's my embellishment for that cloth," Ron says. "You'd be surprised at what the soil could do if you let it be your canvas." He loves that he can walk out his door and be surrounded by nature even in one of the country's largest cities. Bees buzz among the flowers. Birds perch in the trees. People stop in his garden just to stand amid the leaves. A neighbor tells him that the sight of his sunflowers cheers her up. Ron created an oasis of nature in an unlikely place, and he thinks that other people who live in cities can do it, too.

Since that first garden, Ron has helped plant dozens of gardens throughout South Los Angeles, and his work has inspired gardeners around the world. He's shared his story in a TED Talk, and a filmmaker made a documentary about him. He's earned the nickname the "Gangsta Gardener" because in a neighborhood known for its gang violence, Ron envisions a new way to be tough. He also started a nonprofit called the Ron Finley Project to help people plant even more edible gardens in the city.

Los Angeles has 26 square miles of vacant lots. What could happen if those empty lots became gardens? Ron thinks that could change people's lives. "You're changing the ecosystem when you put in a garden," he says. "We are part of the ecosystem so that garden is changing us."

WAYS TO CARE

YOU: Grow Native Plants

If you want to help your hometown's habitat, there's something special you can grow: native plants. A native plant is a species that occurs naturally in a specific place. They're adapted to the local environment and are critical parts of the ecosystem because native insects and animals use them for food and shelter.

Here's how to grow native plants right where you are.

- Research plants that are native to where you live. You can use the Audubon Native Plants Database to find out what they are.

- Choose one or two plants to grow.

- If you have space, plant them in your yard or garden. If you don't have a yard, plant them in a pot and set them outside.

LOCAL: Join a Community Garden

As Ron Finley's story shows, even if you don't have a yard, you can still be a gardener. Schools, community centers, churches, and apartment buildings often have community gardens, where volunteers can grow vegetables. Sometimes the food is grown for the volunteers, and sometimes it is given to local food pantries. Is there a community garden you can be a part of? If not, ask your school or community center about starting one.

GLOBAL: Support Wildlife Crossings

As cities grow, animals have less freedom to move safely from one part of their habitat to the next. Roads are dangerous barriers to wildlife. In Los Angeles in 2012, a mountain lion got stranded in Griffith Park. He had somehow found his way across the freeways to reach this urban oasis, but then he couldn't seem to leave. One solution that could help this mountain lion, and other stranded animals, is wildlife crossings.

A wildlife crossing is a special underpass or overpass that animals can use to cross busy roadways. Amazingly, they work! In some places they've reduced accidents between wildlife and cars by up to 90 percent. Many species use wildlife crossings, including deer, bear, moose, raccoons, foxes, turtles, even salamanders. Is this an idea that would work where you live? Look at a map of your city and think about where you'd design a wildlife crossing. If you can, sketch your idea and share it with your city council and local government.

Emergent

Canopy

Understory

Forest Floor

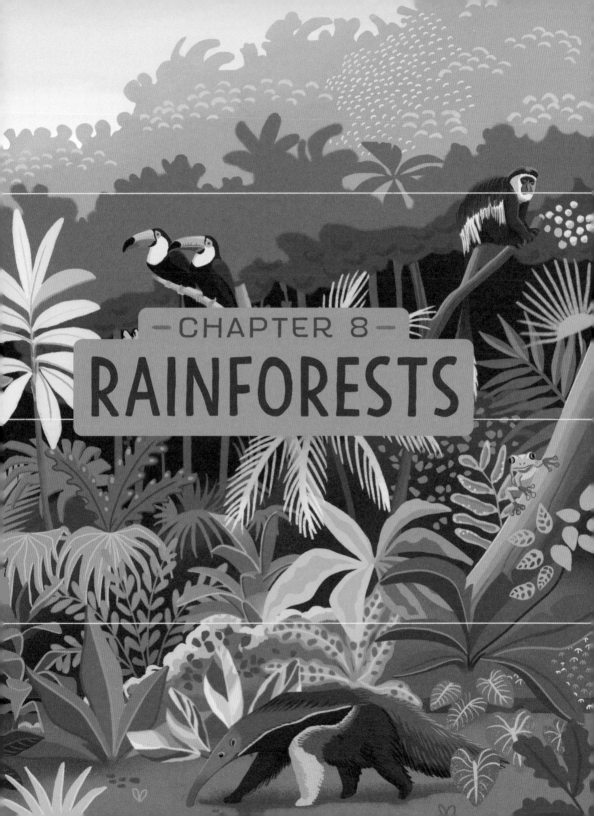

-CHAPTER 8-
RAINFORESTS

Every part of a rainforest seems to be alive. The canopy's leafy branches sway and shudder. The air is filled with rushing rain, buzzing insects, and bird chatter. The forest floor moves with the constant traffic of shiny beetles, scurrying ants, and other creatures that creep and crawl. The rainforest is a crowded and busy habitat, yet everything here—from the tallest kapok tree to the tiniest butterfly—has an important role to play. And together, the rainforest habitat plays an important part in our world. Rainforests store an incredible amount of carbon dioxide, produce oxygen, help regulate the global water cycle, and produce food and medicine.

RAINFOREST FACTS

1. A rainforest is a forest that receives a lot of rainfall each year—anywhere from **60 TO 400 INCHES**!

2. There are two types of rainforests: **TEMPERATE** and **TROPICAL**. Temperate rainforests are usually found near coasts and have cooler temperatures. There are temperate rainforests along North America's Pacific Coast in places like Washington State and British Columbia. Tropical rainforests grow in regions close to the Equator. They receive a lot more rainfall and are hot and humid all year.

3. A rainforest is divided into four layers, from top to bottom: **EMERGENT**, **CANOPY**, **UNDERSTORY**, and **FOREST FLOOR**. Most animals live in the canopy, the second highest layer. That's because most of the food—like flowers, fruit, and insects—is found here.

4. Most trees that grow in rainforests are **EVERGREENS**, meaning they don't shed their leaves every year.

5. Tropical rainforests are packed with diverse plants and wildlife. In just 4 square miles, you can find **400** bird species, **150** butterfly species, and more than **2,000** plant and trees species.

THE RAINFOREST VISIONARY
ALMIR NARAYAMOGA SURUÍ

BORN AUGUST 19, 1974

"Humans can't live without the forest and the forest can't live without humans. Balance is key to nature. Our role is to maintain this equilibrium."

—Almir Narayamoga Suruí

Almir Suruí lay in his hammock inside his family's *maloca* and listened to the rain. His father promised to take him into the forest today. Almir Narayamoga Suruí belonged to the Paiter Suruí, an Indigenous tribe who had lived in the Amazon longer than anyone could remember. His village was at the edge of the rainforest, but he had never been allowed to explore it.

After the rain stopped and the air grew thick and hot, Almir Suruí's father, Marimop, led his son through the trees. Every so often, Marimop stopped and pointed: *The spikes of this palm tree are dangerous, but the fruit is good to eat. If you get hurt, the sap from this liana's bark can stop bleeding. Notice how the forest has gone silent? A jaguar might be near.* There was a lesson every step of the way. Then his father asked, "Do you hear that?" Almir Suruí heard a faint squeak. His father said it was the call of the *cutia*, a large brown rodent. "It means that war will arrive soon," Maripop said. "Your life will be a battle, my son."

People of the Rainforest

More than one million Indigenous peoples live in the Amazon rainforest. Before Almir Suruí was born, there were 5,000 Paiter Suruí. As people from the outside world moved into the Amazon, the Paiter Suruí avoided them as long as possible. But in 1969, everything changed. Maripop and other young men went on a scouting mission and came upon a giant yellow "snake" devouring everything in its path. They ran to stop it and discovered it was controlled by light-skinned men who spoke an unfamiliar language. The snake was a bulldozer, and it would not stop destroying their forest home no matter what they did.

Since the 1600s, colonizers from outside the Amazon had been staking claims to the rainforest, cutting down trees and building rubber plantations, mining operations, palm oil plantations, and cattle ranches. But the people who brought bulldozers did more than destroy trees. They nearly wiped out the Paiter Suruí, and other Indigenous peoples, through disease and violence. By the time Almir

Suruí was born in 1974, there were only 204 Paiter Suruí people left. Nine years later, the Brazilian government finally recognized their 1,000-square-mile territory. But this wasn't the end of their troubles.

Like his ancestors, Almir Suruí grew up speaking Tupi-Monde and was taught how to live in the rainforest. He learned to predict rain, hunt, and make ceremonial paint from the *jenipapo* fruit. As a teenager, he attended meetings with Paiter Suruí chiefs and other Indigenous leaders.

Almir Suruí also learned about the world beyond the Amazon. He studied Portuguese, Brazil's national language. And he saw how Indigenous peoples were hurt by outsiders who came into the rainforest. The Paiter Suruí's territory was still being destroyed by timber poachers, illegal miners, and corrupt government officials who didn't enforce the law. Almir Suruí decided to attend college so he could help his people. In 1992, he graduated with a biology degree and was elected chief of his clan. He was just seventeen years old.

Almir Suruí knew the rainforest was important to the health of the entire world, and that the Amazon's Indigenous peoples played a special part in caring for it. After all, they had lived there sustainably for thousands of years. But he also knew that as long as people could earn money from demolishing the rainforest, they would be unlikely to stop. This gave Almir Suruí an idea: What if people could make money from *saving* the rainforest?

A Brighter Future

The new chief had big dreams. In just a few years he helped his people build a medical clinic, create a school for children to learn Tupi-Monde and Portuguese, and reconnect to their culture. But he had other goals that would take more time. He wanted to create ways for the Paiter Suruí to preserve the rainforest and earn income through organic farming, ecotourism, and conservation.

Almir Suruí discovered a way that technology could help. In 2003, he saw satellite photos of the Paiter Suruí's territory on Google Earth. Two things shocked him. First, Google Earth had no information about indigenous territories—it was as if they didn't exist. He also saw huge deforested areas, both outside and inside Paiter Suruí land. He wondered if his people could use Google Earth to track illegal logging and report it to the Brazilian government.

Almir Suruí traveled to Google headquarters in California to ask if they would partner with him. They agreed. Google sent a team to teach the Paiter Suruí how to use computers, smartphones, and cameras to track illegal logging. The tribe also started using the technology to record their territory's biodiversity and cultural information.

A Work in Progress

In addition to being rainforest protectors, the Paiter Suruí are restoring what's been lost. Almir Suruí set a goal of planting one million trees in deforested areas. So far, they've planted more than 700,000. The restoration work helped earn income, just as Almir Suruí hoped. In 2009, he helped create the Suruí Forest Carbon Project to help businesses make up for the carbon they produce by paying the Paiter Suruí to plant trees in the rainforest.

Almir Suruí's bold ideas have received international praise, but they've also put him in danger. Timber poachers put a bounty on his head, and he must travel with bodyguards. In 2019, things took a turn for the worse in Brazil with the election of a president who refuses to protect the rainforest and does not respect the rights of Indigenous people.

Yet Almir Suruí keeps working for the good of his people and the rainforest. To understand why, it might help to read a Paiter Suruí story that Almir Suruí tells his children:

One day, a huge fire swept across the rainforest. All the animals had fled except one hummingbird that kept on and wouldn't stop carrying water in his beak to douse the trees on fire.

"What are you doing, little bird?" an armadillo asked him. "You can't think that you are going to stop the fire with just the water in your beak!"

The hummingbird remained focused on his work. "I know very well that I won't stop the fire all by myself, but at least I will have done my part."

THE WORLD'S
OLDEST RAINFOREST

To understand ancient plants and animals, people usually dig deep into the ground or crack open rocks to reveal fossils inside. But there's one part of the world where ancient plants still grow green in the forest's shadows and ancient animals leave fresh footprints in the dirt: the **WET TROPICS OF QUEENSLAND**. That's where you'll find the world's oldest continuously surviving rainforests.

The Wet Tropics of Queensland, a region in northeastern Australia, is 3,400 square miles and include 31 national parks and state forests. There are species here that have hardly changed since their Jurassic ancestors roamed the Earth. The Wet Tropics also have a long human history. They're home to 18 Aboriginal tribal groups, including the Eastern Kuku Yalanji people, who have lived there for thousands of years. The Eastern Kuku Yalanji are the traditional owners of Daintree National Park.

Queensland's rainforests are only a small part of Australia—just 0.3 percent—but are rich with plants and animals. More than 40 percent of Australia's bird species, 60 percent of its butterfly species, and 35 percent of its mammal species live here. The region's biodiversity is one reason it was named a UNESCO World Heritage Site in 2012. Here are some of its amazing plants and animals:

The **WAIT-A-WHILE** is a climbing palm with long, sharp spikes. Its name comes from its tendency to get caught in people's clothing as they pass by.

CHINGIA AUSTRALIS is an endangered filmy fern species. The leaves are thin and fragile—just one cell thick (about the thickness of an onion skin!).

The **MOUNTAIN BLUE BUTTERFLY** (or Ulysses Butterfly) has iridescent blue wings. Its favorite food is the flowers of the Pink Flowered Doughwood tree.

GOLDEN ORB SPIDERS are harmless to humans. Their name comes from the beautiful golden webs they weave.

BOYD'S FOREST DRAGON is a lizard that lives only in the Queensland rainforest. It perches on tree trunks to ambush its prey: ants, grasshoppers, beetles, and earthworms.

BENNETT'S TREE KANGAROO is a shy marsupial—and a cousin of the kangaroo—that lives in the treetops.

The **CASSOWARY** is a huge flightless bird and one of the most important animal species in these rainforests. More than 100 plant species depend on the cassowary to spread the seeds of their fruits that it eats.

The **DOUBLE-EYED FIG PARROT** got its name because figs are usually the only food it eats. It's Australia's smallest parrot, at just $5\frac{1}{2}$ inches tall.

The tiny **BLOSSOM BAT** loves flower nectar and pollen. Even though these bats are barely 2 inches long, they're powerful pollinators, spreading six times the amount of pollen as birds.

BE A FIELD BIOLOGIST

To be a rainforest researcher or an artist who works in the wild, it helps to have a sense of adventure. But there's something else you need: patience. To really see nature, you have to stay still. When you're constantly moving, it's easy to trample or scare away the things you're trying to observe. Whether you want to be a botanical artist like Margaret Mee (page 194) or a field biologist who discovers a new frog species, nature observation is a good skill to practice.

You don't have to join a rainforest expedition—you can do it right where you live. First, choose an outdoor location that you can visit a few times in a row, such as a spot in your yard or at a park. If there isn't a comfortable place to sit, bring a chair. (If you're unable to go outside, you can also look out of a window whose view includes a tree, garden, or other green space.) You should be able to sit in this spot for at least 15 minutes, which will give wild creatures time to get used to your presence. Return to this spot 4 or 5 times on different days. On each visit, be as still and as quiet as you can. Then write down these observations in your field notebook:

LOCATION AND DATE:
Note where you are, plus the date and time.

_____

WEATHER: Is it sunny and windy? Cloudy and foggy?
Write down everything you notice about the weather.

_____

ONE THING YOU SEE: This can be anything from a specific insect
to a certain shade of green.

_____

ONE THING YOU HEAR: It might help to close your eyes so you
can focus better.

_____

ONE THING YOU FEEL: This can be something like the sun on
your face or something you can touch with your hand, like dried pine
needles or rough tree bark.

_____

SOMETHING THAT'S THE SAME FROM YOUR LAST
VISIT: Notice what stays the same from visit to visit.

_____

SOMETHING THAT'S DIFFERENT FROM YOUR LAST
VISIT: Notice what changes from visit to visit. Has anything grown
larger or changed color? Is something missing that was there before?

_____

When you take time to be still and quiet, you can make surprising
discoveries about the natural world.

_____

PERU'S LOST WORLD

For a long time, the **CORDILLERA AZUL RAINFOREST** was a blank spot on Peru's map. This mountainous rainforest is the size of Connecticut, but it's protected by steep cliffs like the walls of a fortress. Few people had ever explored it. Even the indigenous people who lived nearby didn't venture far into it. But in the 1990s, this rainforest faced its first real threat. Logging and mining operations cut down the trees around it, then set their sights on Cordillera Azul. Conservationists urged Peru's government to protect the land, but they needed to prove the region was worth saving.

In 1996, scientists embarked on the first expedition into the Cordillera Azul rainforest. The journey took days by boat, followed by days of hiking through the jungle. There were no roads or trails. The scientists spent two months exploring and writing down what they found. At first, Cordillera Azul seemed like other rainforests they'd seen. Mighty trees blocked sunlight and every square inch was packed with plant life. Herds of peccaries roamed the forest floor, bird calls echoed through the air, and curious monkeys—who had never seen a human—cautiously crept down from the trees. But the scientists also realized that this place was like a "lost world," home to species unknown to science.

Four years later, a second expedition continued the research. Now the clock was ticking. Logging companies had applied for permits. A team of Peruvian and American scientists took a helicopter into the heart of the rainforest. In six weeks, the researchers recorded more than 1,800 animal and plant species—including new species of birds, frogs, fish, and a squirrel! The scientists delivered their report to the Peruvian government. With scientific data to support their decision, the government quickly made plans to protect Cordillera Azul. In May

2001, President Valentin Panagua signed a law creating Cordillera Azul National Park, a wilderness that stretches more than 5,000 square miles.

People have been destroying the world's rainforests for a long time. The story of Cordillera Azul shows what can happen when people work together to protect them instead. Here are some plants and animals that now live in peace in Cordillera Azul:

SCARLET-BANDED BARBET

VIOLET-HEADED HUMMINGBIRD

CORDILLERA AZUL ANTBIRD

WHITE CATFISH

AMAZON DWARF SQUIRREL

BUSH DOG

PERUVIAN SPIDER MONKEY

CACAO TREE

WILD BIRDNEST FERN

MAKE A RAINFOREST BIOME

A rainforest is a hardworking ecosystem. It even creates its own rain! Some tropical rainforests can create up to 75 percent of their own rainfall. To see how this works, grow a rainforest in a jar!

Supplies

1-quart glass jar with a lid

1 5-by- 5-inch square of mesh screen

Marker

Scissors

$\frac{3}{4}$ cup aquarium gravel

$\frac{1}{4}$ cup activated charcoal

1 cup tropical potting soil

1 to 2 small tropical plants

3 tablespoons distilled water

Instructions

1. Set the jar on top of the mesh screen. Trace around the bottom of the jar with the marker, then cut out the mesh circle.

2. Pour the gravel into the jar. Then put the mesh circle on top of the gravel. The gravel will be the water reservoir.

3. Spread the charcoal on top of the mesh. The charcoal will filter water as it drains into the reservoir. Spread the potting soil over the charcoal.

4. Make a small hole in the soil. Place a plant into the hole so its roots are inside. Cover the roots with soil. Repeat with other plants.

5. Pour the distilled water into the jar. Then

seal the jar with the lid. Place the terrarium near a sunny spot (but not in direct sunlight). The jar should have condensation on the inside in the morning and evening. If the jar has condensation all the time, it needs to air out. Remove the lid until the condensation goes away, then put the lid back on. If condensation doesn't form after the first couple days, add 1–2 tablespoons of distilled water.

Caring for Your Rainforest

Your rainforest will take care of itself! You'll likely only need to add a few tablespoons of water a couple times a year. That's because this terrarium mimics the water cycle of a real rainforest. The water you added will soak into the soil and hydrate the plants. Excess water will drain into the gravel. Next, the water in the reservoir will evaporate and condense on the sides of the jar. Then the condensation (water droplets) will fall into the soil to water the plants—and the cycle will begin again.

THE INTREPID ARTIST
MARGARET MEE

MAY 22, 1909–NOVEMBER 30, 1988

"My close contact with the vast forests and waterways of the Amazon had given me an overwhelming desire to go back for further discoveries and inspiration."

—Margaret Mee

No one had ever painted a moonflower in full bloom. The flower bloomed only once in the middle of the night, and then it was gone. Margaret had spent twenty years searching for a wild moonflower to paint. She followed rumors of the plant along the Amazon River where its vines twisted around trees. She'd seen the plant's fruit and leaves. But somehow, she always missed the flower. Now on her fifteenth Amazon expedition, at age seventy-nine, she hoped at last to see one.

The flooded rainforest grew dark, and a night chorus of birds and frogs filled the air. Tree branches reached up through the water like arms stretching to the sky. Margaret sat very still in a canoe. She could see a moonflower bud sprouting from a vine right in front of her! It was as white as the moon and closed tightly like a fist. Margaret began to sketch.

From England to Brazil

Margaret Mee was born in Chesham, England in 1909. She went to art school and worked as a professional artist for many years until a trip to South America changed her life. In the early 1950s, Margaret visited her sister in São Paulo; she loved Brazil so much that she decided to stay and teach art. Her husband, Greville, joined her from England and they bought a small house. From the start, Margaret was in awe of Brazil's tropical plants. She sketched and painted them whenever she could and let them run wild in her back garden.

In 1956, Margaret and a teacher friend of hers traveled for the first time to the Amazon to paint its incredible plants. The pair didn't quite know what they were getting into. They wore the wrong clothing (heavy jeans and thick cotton shirts) and didn't bring enough supplies.

It was a long trip from São Paulo to the Amazon. They flew in a cargo plane, then rode a slow-moving train that spit sparks and smoke, and then took two unreliable boats. The first was a wooden launch packed with seasick people;

the second was a canoe with a sputtering motor. When the rain poured, the two women wrapped themselves in plastic sheets, and at night they slept in hammocks. Despite the trip's challenges, Margaret returned home knowing one thing: she wanted to go back.

Artist and Activist

Margaret returned to the Amazon every few years, spending up to four months seeking out and sketching plants. Sometimes she stayed with Indigenous people. Other times she stayed in a borrowed hut with only a boat pilot and assistant for company. Margaret preferred to sketch plants in their natural habitat. With the rainforest's ever-changing weather and undependable transportation, she often had to sketch in a hurry. Sometimes she collected specimens to bring home for Brazilian botanists.

When Margaret wasn't in the Amazon, she taught younger botanical illustrators and was a researcher for the São Paulo Botanic Institute. She became well known in Brazil for her botanical paintings and plant-collecting skills; some of the species she discovered were named in her honor. After a respected botanist hired Margaret to illustrate one of his books, scientists around the world began to take notice of her incredible art.

Although Margaret had a firsthand look at the wonder of Brazil's rainforests, she also saw the devastation. On each new expedition, she witnessed trees being cleared for farming, mining, and roads. Instead of the lush forests she remembered, Margaret floated past acres of burned stumps. The destruction made Margaret want to take action, and so she did.

As a young woman in England, Margaret found it easy to raise her voice. She had joined protests and gave bold speeches for causes she cared about. Now she raised her voice for the rainforest. She wrote a report about how deforestation was harming the people, plants, and animals and sent it to Brazil's department of forestry. She wrote letters and met with government officials.

Margaret also used her art to show people what was being lost. When she painted plants, she included some of their surroundings. She wanted viewers to understand that plants don't exist alone but as part of a complex habitat. The loss of the rainforest motivated Margaret to keep exploring and to find as many plants as she could. She wanted to share them with the world before they were gone. One of her last quests was to find the moonflower.

A Final Expedition

A nearly eighty-year-old Margaret sat in a canoe in the middle of the night. A friend pointed her flashlight beam at the moonflower bud, making sure they didn't miss it. But they hardly needed the light. The moon above shone like a bright pearl. Then, as Margaret watched, the flower began to bloom. She saw its white petals spiral open like a pale firework. She sketched quickly, capturing the flower at every stage, from tight bud to withered blossom. Hours later, as morning brightened the sky, Margaret finished her sketches. "With the dawn the flower closed," she later wrote, "and we watched, fascinated and humbled by the experience."

WAYS TO CARE

YOU: Pay Attention to Palm Oil

Even if you live thousands of miles from a rainforest, the products you use can help it or hurt it. One of the biggest reasons rainforests are cut down is to grow oil palm trees. Palm oil is in many products, including shampoo, ice cream, and biofuel. (Sometimes palm oil appears on ingredients lists as vegetable oil, palm kernel oil, palmate, or sodium kernelate.) But the solution is not as simple as boycotting palm oil. For now, the best solution is to support companies that produce it in more rainforest-friendly ways. Look for products that have a seal from the RSPO (Roundtable on Sustainable Palm Oil).

LOCAL: Support Rainforest Conservation

Janine Licare moved to Costa Rica when she was four years old. When she saw her local rainforest being cut down, she wanted to do something about it. With her mom's help, Janine and a friend started a nonprofit called Kids Saving the Rainforest (KSTR) when she was only nine years old. More than twenty years later, KSTR is still going strong. The organization has built a wildlife sanctuary for injured and orphaned animals and an education center and is replanting trees in a 300-acre section of Costa Rican rainforest. Schools all over the world hold fundraisers to support their work. Here are some projects your school could raise money to support:

PLANT TREES in the local Costa Rican rainforest

SPONSOR A TITI MONKEY in the wildlife sanctuary

BUILD WILDLIFE BRIDGES that protect endangered monkeys from roads and powerlines

SPONSOR A SLOTH in the wildlife sanctuary

GLOBAL: Start the Conversation

Businesses have the power to help or hurt rainforests. It's good to remember that businesses are run by people, and people can change their minds. If a company uses palm oil or wood that's harvested in unsustainable ways, the public should tell them why that's harmful. At the same time, when businesses make rainforest-friendly decisions, it's important to encourage their good work. Write a letter or email to a business that's currently hurting the rainforests and a business that's helping them.

When you write to a company you should include:

- Your age

- Why rainforests matter. You may want to share facts you've learned or include some art you've created or photos you've found.

- What you'd like
  the company to do
  differently and why you
  think it's a good idea–
  or thank them for the
  ways they're helping.

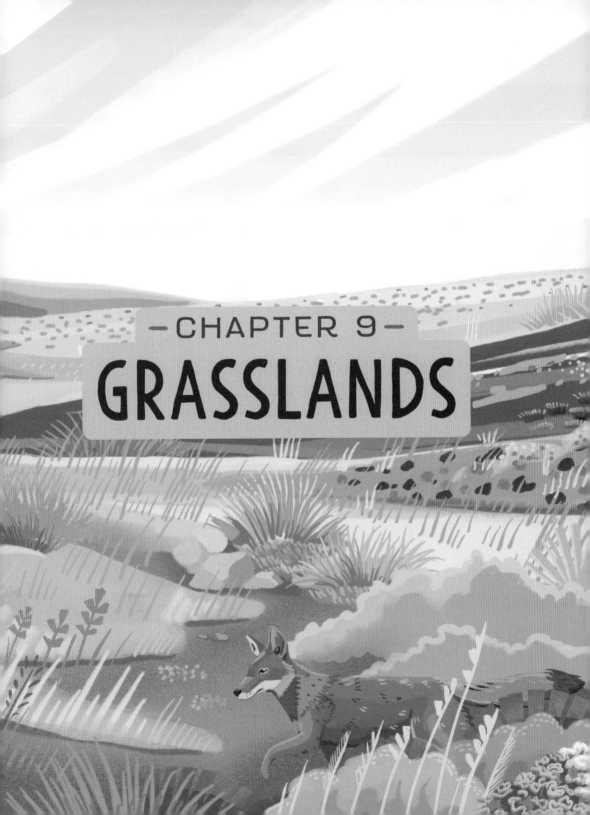

—CHAPTER 9—
GRASSLANDS

There are places in the world where grass stretches to the horizon like a rippling sea. Where grasses grow so tall, they can hide an elephant herd or pride of lions. And there are places where grass grows in small meadows or forgotten fields. Grass is a familiar plant to most people. It's so common that it's easy to miss how special it is. It grows in yards, parks, roadside ditches—it even sprouts through cracks in the sidewalk. Grasslands are a natural habitat where grass and grass-like plants grow in large numbers. They need less rain than forests but more rain than deserts. And grasses are really good at growing.

⇶ GRASSLANDS FACTS ⇷

1. Every continent except Antarctica has grasslands, but they have different names depending on where they are in the world: **GRASSLANDS**, **PRAIRIES**, or **MEADOWS** (North America), **PAMPAS** or **LLANOS** (South America), **MEADOWS** or **STEPPES** (Europe and Asia), **SAVANNAS** or **VELDTS** (Africa), or **RANGELANDS** (Australia).

2. Northern India has some of the world's tallest grasslands. Grasses there can grow more than **9 FEET** high. Huge animals like Asian elephants and wild water buffalo live and eat in these tall swaying grasses.

3. Grass is one of the fastest growing plants in the world. Some species grow nearly **2 FEET** in a single day!

4. Grasslands can support many different animal species. Most animals who live in grasslands are **NOMADIC**, meaning that they're always on the move as they graze or search for food.

5. **FIRE** might be harmful to other types of habitats, but most grasslands need fire to be healthy ecosystems. Fires destroy dead plant material that could interfere with new seeds reaching the soil and new shoots reaching the sun.

THE POETIC SCIENTIST
ROBIN WALL KIMMERER
BORN 1953

"How we think about our relationship to the living world matters deeply."

—Robin Wall Kimmerer

R obin had been waiting for the wild strawberries. In May she searched the meadows behind her house. She found their new leaves and the white flowers that bloomed and fell like stars. Tiny fruit formed, bright green ripening to pink as the weeks passed. By early June, the evening air was warm and sweet, and the pale *ode'mini-giizis*, Strawberry Moon, shone through the trees. It was time.

Robin ran home from the bus stop on her last day of school. She changed her clothes and dashed out the back door, walking through the thick meadow grasses and climbing an old stone wall. The pale pink strawberries had turned to rubies in the early summer heat. Robin picked a handful, and their bright sweetness burst in her mouth. In the Potawatomi language, strawberries are called *ode min*, which means "heart berries." It's similar to their word for "gift." To Robin and Potawatomi people, the wild strawberries were one of the Earth's gifts. And as a future botanist, they were also one of Robin's first teachers.

A Born Botanist

Robin Wall Kimmerer followed her love of nature from the wild meadows to the classroom. By the time she went to college in the 1970s, she had spent years studying plants on her own. She collected seeds in shoeboxes and preserved leaves between pages of books. As a college student, she studied botany and ecology. She read textbooks and observed plants in the lab and field. But she also had questions that science couldn't answer. She wanted to know why certain stems could bend and be used for basket-making but others were brittle and snapped. She wondered why goldenrod and asters looked beautiful together growing in the meadow. But her questions were dismissed. One botany professor told her: "If you want to study beauty, you should go to art school." Robin kept studying. She became an expert on mosses. She earned her doctorate degree and became a college professor. Yet something was missing.

Robin's grandfather Asa Wall was a member of the Citizen Potawatomi Nation. He was born in Oklahoma. But as a young boy, Asa was sent to the Carlisle Indian School in Pennsylvania, where he was forced to give up his Native language and culture. He never went home again. Instead, he made a life for himself in rural New York. By the time Robin was a child, her family was reconnecting with Potawatomi people and culture, but there was much she didn't know. Robin's love of plants would help lead her back to the Indigenous knowledge her grandfather had been forced to leave behind.

Goldenrod and Asters

When she was a new professor, Robin went to a gathering of Native elders who were meeting to discuss their traditional knowledge of plants. One elder, a Navajo woman, had no formal training in botany but her knowledge about plants was deeper and wider than anything Robin had learned. The woman spoke in great detail about the plants where she lived. Not only their names, where they grew, and the shapes of their leaves, but also their origin stories and what they can teach people.

Robin realized this is what had been missing in her work as a scientist. She always thought she had to choose between two ways of understanding nature: science or Indigenous knowledge. From then on, she used her research and writing to bring the two strands together. They reminded her of the yellow goldenrod and purple asters in the meadow, two different plants that thrived when they grew side by side.

Science had taught Robin to be a detached observer, to look at plants as if they were objects separate from her own experience. But according to Potawatomi beliefs, all living things—including plants, animals, and people—are connected. The relationships between living things matter. Robin realized that many of the world's environmental problems were the result of a broken relationship between people and nature. It had become normal for people to take from nature without giving back. People were used to seeing things in nature—trees, water, even wild strawberries—as goods to buy and sell and consume. But in Potawatomi culture, things in nature are seen as gifts. And because people receive gifts from nature, they have a responsibility to nature.

Robin began to teach college courses that combined science and Indigenous knowledge. In 2006, she became founding director of the Center for Native Peoples and the Environment at the State University of New York in Syracuse. The Center offers classes where students combine Indigenous knowledge with scientific tools to help solve environmental problems. It also works to create more opportunities for Native students in environmental science. Unlike when Robin was in college, these students are encouraged to bring their culture into the classroom.

Healing the Land

It's a warm summer day and Robin is planting sweetgrass in a meadow. She digs into the soil and places a clump in the hole. She welcomes the plant, then taps around its roots. In the surrounding meadow, graduate students and members of the Mohawk community are doing the same thing. Robin is now a conservation leader and writer who focuses on ecological restoration. But her work is about more than restoring nature; she also endeavors to restore Indigenous culture.

In the meadow along the Mohawk River, she and her students are replanting sweetgrass—one of the four sacred plants of the Potawatomi and a sacred plant of the Mohawk. Two centuries after being forced from their ancestral lands in New York, a small group of Mohawk people returned in 1993. In the Kanatsiohareke Mohawk Community, members are restoring the land and their relationship to it. The sweetgrass will be good for the ecosystem, and it will be used to revive important cultural practices like planting, harvesting, and basket-making. With those things comes the restoration of community. "We can put our hands into the earth, restoring the damage that we have done, healing the land the way the plants have shown us to," Robin says. "It's not the land that's broken, but our relationship to land. We can heal that, you and I together. It starts by asking ourselves: 'What will I give in return for the gifts of the earth?'"

THE SERENGETI

The **SERENGETI PLAINS OF TANZANIA** are some of the most famous grasslands in the world. These lands in eastern Africa feed wildebeest herds, hide lions on the hunt, and are crisscrossed with crocodile-filled rivers. The grasslands here are savannas, a type of grassy habitat that has some scattered trees. The Serengeti plains are also dotted with rocky outcroppings called kopjes (*COP-eez*), the perfect lookout for a pride of hungry lions or a hiding place for a rock hyrax.

The Serengeti has rainy seasons twice a year when the plains turn lush and green, followed by long dry seasons. The rhythm of flood and drought is why the animals in the Serengeti are always on the move. Grazing animals move north to find fresh grass when the drought arrives and south again when the rains return. It's one of the world's largest animal migrations, with 1.5 million wildebeests, 750,000 zebras, and hundreds of thousands of other grazing animals. Predators like lions, leopards, and spotted hyenas are quick to follow.

Because so many creatures depend on it, the Serengeti needs protection from human development. Eighty percent of the region is now protected by parks and reserves, including Serengeti National Park. Some wildlife is thriving here, but others such as the black rhino are endangered because of habitat loss and illegal poaching. The Serengeti has 300 mammal species and 500 bird species, plus reptiles, insects, and plants. Here are some of them.

AFRICAN LION: The Serengeti is home to Africa's largest lion population—more than 3,000. These members of the cat family spend up to 20 hours a day sleeping.

BLUE WILDEBEEST: The horned wildebeest looks like it's related to cattle, but it's a type of large antelope. Despite its size, it can run up to 50 m.p.h.!

FISCHER'S LOVEBIRD: This colorful parrot gets its name from the strong bond that's formed between pairs. They live in small flocks and eat seeds and fruit.

ROCK HYRAX: This furry mammal looks like a large guinea pig, but it's a distant cousin of the elephant. They live in rocky places like the *kopjes* of the Serengeti.

UMBRELLA TREE: This umbrella-shaped tree is a type of acacia tree. Acacias are sometimes called thorn trees because they have sharp barbs to discourage animals from eating their leaves.

RHODES GRASS: This common grass throughout Africa and the Serengeti can grow up to nine feet tall.

FINDING FLOWERS

Grasslands are home to incredible **WILDFLOWERS**. A wildflower is a flowering plant species that's uncultivated, meaning that it has grown and developed without human help or interference. Wildflowers usually have soft stems and can bloom during different times of the year. They also grow in diverse habitats, such as shady forests, deserts, ditches, and windswept grasslands.

What's the difference between a wildflower and a weed? Only your opinion! Wildflowers are considered weeds when they grow in places where people don't want them or when they crowd out other plant species. Dandelions, milkweed, and violets are often considered weeds, but technically they're wildflowers that are really good at growing and spreading. Take a wildflower field trip where you live and see what's blooming. Bring along a wildflower field guide or app, and use the following clues to help you identify the wildflowers you find.

COLOR: The first step in identifying a wildflower is noticing its color. In most field guides and apps, wildflowers are grouped according to the color of their blooms.

SEASON: What month is it? This can be a big clue. There are some flowers that bloom only in certain seasons.

SIZE: What size is the bloom? Is it larger or smaller than others you've seen?

FLOWER SHAPE: Does the plant produce single flowers or clusters of flowers? Single flowers can often be disc-shaped or look like bells or tubes. Flower clusters can be round, flat, or shaped like spikes.

LEAF SHAPE: Wildflower leaves can be a few different shapes such as simple, lobed, compound, or leaflets.

LEAF ATTACHMENT: Notice how the leaves are attached to the stem. Are leaves attached opposite each other along the stem or do they alternate? Or do the leaves grow from one central point?

Common Wildflowers

Here are some of the most common wildflowers in the United States. Some are native to North America and some were brought from other continents. Do any of these wildflowers grow where you live?

OXEYE DAISY (*Leucanthemum vulgare*)

BLACK-EYED SUSAN (*Rudbeckia hirta*)

COMMON SUNFLOWER (*Helianthus annuus*)

COMMON YARROW (*Achillea millefolium*)

DANDELION (*Taraxacum officinale*)

If you live near prairies or meadows, you might see some of these common North American prairie wildflowers.

AROMATIC ASTER (*Aster oblongifolius*)

COMMON MILKWEED (*Asclepias syriaca*)

WILD BERGAMOT (*Monarda fistulosa*)

PURPLE CONEFLOWER (*Echinacea angustifolia*)

COMPASS PLANT (*Silphium laciniatum*)

THE AMERICAN
PRAIRIE RESERVE

In the heart of North America, there was once a grassland as vast and vibrant as Africa's Serengeti. From the Missouri River to the Rocky Mountains, tall-grass, mixed-grass, and shortgrass **PRAIRIES** stretched to the horizon. There were elk, antelope, and bison everywhere. Before European settlement, an estimated 50 million bison roamed the prairies, and their powerful stampedes shook the earth like thunder. But they weren't alone.

For generations, Native American people including the Lakota and Assiniboine lived in these grasslands. The bison was an animal they respected and revered, and it was their most important food source. In the late 1800s, when the U.S. government wanted to force Native Americans off their land and onto reservations, federal officials allowed hunters to hunt the bison to near extinction. Since that time, most of America's original prairie habitats have been turned into farmland or cattle ranches.

But in the northern Great Plains, a shortgrass prairie is being restored. Called the American Prairie Reserve, it's the largest prairie restoration project in the United States. Since 2001, the American Prairie Reserve has been buying former ranching land and working to reestablish plants and animals. America's grasslands were once home to bison, pronghorn, elk, prairie dogs, grizzly bears, and wolves. In time, the conservationists hope that most, if not all, of these species will live again in the reserve.

The American Prairie Reserve is privately owned but is open to anyone who wants to hike, camp, paddle, hunt, and explore. In 2014, the reserve hosted a special ceremony with the Assiniboine and Gros Ventre people who live on the neighboring land. Together, they released 73 young bison to join the existing herd. The young bison were direct descendants of those that once lived on the American prairies. As a group of Assiniboine and Gros Ventre high school students swung open the gate, the animals sprinted into the open prairie and didn't look back, their hooves shaking the earth like thunder.

Here are some of the animals that currently live in this restored prairie habitat.

AMERICAN BISON: Bison can survive the extreme weather of the prairies, including blizzards and droughts.

PRAIRIE DOG: This ground squirrel lives in underground burrows and has a warning call that sounds like a bark.

PRONGHORN: These hoofed animals look like antelope but they're not related. The pronghorn's closest living relative is the giraffe.

BURROWING OWL: This threatened species uses abandoned prairie dog burrows for their own homes.

WHITE-TAILED JACKRABBIT: Also called a prairie hare, this nocturnal rabbit can run up to 34 m.p.h. and leap up to 16 feet!

BOTANICAL ART

Flowers and plants are nature's art supplies. People have been using them to create and decorate for centuries. Archeologists have found dried-flower garlands in ancient Egyptian tombs, and in Japan making pictures with pressed flowers has been an art form since the 1500s. It's called *Oshibana*, which means "pressed flowers." To try it yourself, collect some fresh flowers or plants. Pick plants from your own garden or from someone who has given you permission. Also, make sure you know what plant you're picking so you know it's safe to touch.

Supplies

Fresh flowers or
    plants

White printer paper

Heavy books

Instructions

1. Fold a piece of printer paper in half. Open it and lay it flat, then arrange a few flowers or leaves on one half.

2. Carefully refold the paper with the plants inside. Make sure the leaves and petals are flat and not touching. Place the folded paper between the pages of a heavy book.

3. Repeat steps 1 and 2 using more plants. You can place each folded paper in the same book several pages apart.

4. Store the book where it won't be disturbed, and place more heavy books on top.

5. After two weeks, check the plants to see if they're dried and flattened. If they're not, wait another week. Once the plants are completely dry and flat, use them for one of the following crafts.

Bookmark

Using heavy watercolor paper, cut out a 2-by-6-inch rectangle. Use a foam brush to apply a thin layer of Mod Podge to one side of the rectangle. Place pressed plants on top and let dry. Then cover the plants with 1 to 2 coats of Mod Podge and let dry.

Wall Art

Cut an 8-by-10-inch rectangle from a piece of cardstock. Arrange pressed plants on the paper in any design you choose. Pick up one plant at a time and dab a few spots of clear craft glue on the cardstock where you want to attach it. Press the plant in place. Repeat until all the plants are glued down. Let dry. Then frame your artwork.

Rocks

Use a foam brush to cover a smooth stone with Mod Podge. While the rock is still wet, attach pressed flowers and leaves to the surface. Smooth out wrinkles and let dry. Then use the foam brush to cover the rock with 1 to 2 more coats of Mod Podge. Let dry.

THE INNOVATIVE BOTANIST

GEORGE WASHINGTON CARVER

1864–JANUARY 5, 1943

"Much of our success in orchard, field, and garden will depend on the closeness with which we stick to nature's laws in the way of giving to each plant its proper environment."

—George Washington Carver

W hen George was a child, he collected specimens from nature: a striped rock, a quail feather, a papery snakeskin. He brought them home to the his family's log cabin and lined them up in rows. Plant specimens were his favorite. George knew more about plants than most people. The neighbors called him "the plant doctor." In a way, that's what George would one day become: a botanist.

From Art to Science

George Washington Carver was born in 1864 near Diamond Grove, Missouri. A white couple named Moses and Susan Carver had enslaved his mother, Mary, and older brother Jim. Mary died tragically when George was still a baby. When slavery was abolished in the United States the next year, George and Jim had nowhere to go. The Carvers—who had no children of their own—raised the two boys. George was often sick throughout his childhood, so he was excused from farm chores. Instead, he explored the outdoors alone. "I wanted to know every strange stone, flower, insect, bird, or beast," he later wrote. "I wanted to know where it got its color, where it got its life—but there was no one to tell me."

When George was thirteen years old, he attended a school for Black students in a nearby town and stayed with Andrew and Mariah Watkins, a Black couple who lived near the school. Ms. Watkins told George, "You must learn all you can, then go back out into the world and give your learning back to the people." In 1885, George was accepted to college but when school officials saw that he was Black, they changed their minds.

Five years later, George enrolled in Simpson College in Iowa and planned to become a painter. An art teacher was impressed by his knowledge of plants, however, and suggested that he become an agricultural scientist. George transferred to the Iowa Agricultural School (later, Iowa State University) and began to dream about how he could use agricultural science to help other Black people.

The Plant Professor

In the late 1800s, the farm fields of the Southern United States were worn out from growing cotton. If the same type of plant is grown over and over in the same place, the soil's nutrients get used up and plants struggle to grow. That's what was happening to the Southern farms. Black farmers were especially affected. Many were sharecroppers, which meant they rented their farms from white landlords. With such poor soil, the sharecroppers couldn't grow enough crops to get out of debt. George had a strong Christian faith and became convinced that his life's purpose was to use agricultural science to help Black farmers.

After earning his master's degree in botany at Iowa Agricultural School—the first Black person to do so—he received a prestigious job offer. Tuskegee Institute (today known as Tuskegee University) is a college for Black students in Alabama. In 1896, the school's president, Booker T. Washington, hired George to be the head of its agriculture department. His responsibilities included teaching, research, managing the school's farms (more than 2,300 acres), and running an agricultural experiment station.

On campus, George developed an eccentric reputation. He made his own clothes and wore a wildflower tucked into his lapel. He sometimes foraged for his meals. His teaching style was unique, too. His lectures combined various subjects—botany, geology, literature, and art—and he didn't teach only in the classroom. George taught his students outdoors. Using a sweet potato or a flower as a prop, he explained that nature was made up of relationships between living things.

George shared his knowledge with people outside the school, too. He wrote bulletins (printed paper pamphlets) to teach the public. In all, George wrote forty-four bulletins on such subjects as how to restore depleted soil, how to grow peanuts, and how to include nature in public education. George chose his words carefully. He wanted people who had little to no education to understand the information. He also taught farmers in the community with a mobile classroom he constructed on a horse-drawn wagon.

Ahead of His Time

When people think of George Washington Carver today, many think about peanuts. One of his bulletins included 105 recipes for peanuts, and he once testified before Congress on behalf of the peanut industry. Along with being a botanist and professor, he was an inventor. He promoted peanuts, sweet potatoes, and soybeans as cash crops that could replace cotton. (And they did.) He invented 300 products made from peanuts, including peanut flour, paint, and shampoo. George became world famous for his scientific work.

George was a lifelong naturalist and a conservationist who was ahead of his time. He spent his life sharing his love of nature and encouraging others to think about how humans affect the places where they live and work, especially when growing food. Many of his ideas about how to live and farm in sustainable ways would only become popular decades after he died. Looking back over his own life, George once said, "My work is that of conservation."

WAYS TO CARE

YOU: Grow a Pocket Prairie

Even a small grassland habitat—a pocket prairie—can make a difference for the wildlife that needs it. Find out which wildflowers and grasses are native to your area and plant some in your yard or in pots. When the growing season is over, collect seeds to plant next year. If you want to help grasslands on a bigger scale, see if your school will organize a prairie-planting project. In 2019, fourth graders from three elementary schools in Chatham, Illinois, planted a 10-acre prairie next to one of their schools!

LOCAL AND GLOBAL: Food for Thought

With rich soil and regular rainfall, grassland habitat is one of the best places to grow food. That's why so many grasslands have been plowed up for farmland. Farming is hard work that's full of challenges like destructive insects, weeds, weather, and changing laws and markets. Many modern farming solutions hurt the environment by using up land and water and creating pollution.

Yet we all need to eat, and the food has to come from somewhere. Is it possible to feed the world without damaging the environment? Today farmers, scientists, and researchers are answering that question. Here are some eco-friendly farming methods that people have developed.

ORGANIC FARMING: Organic farmers use methods that are good for the soil, water, and air, such as rotating crops (to let the soil recover), avoiding toxic chemicals, and providing pasture for livestock.

AGROFORESTRY: In the past, cutting down trees was a common way to prepare a field for crops. But it turns out that agroforestry—growing the right trees alongside crops or livestock—can be good for farmers and the ecosystem. Some farmers use trees to reduce soil erosion, produce natural fertilizer, keep more water in the soil, and absorb carbon dioxide.

HYDROPONICS, AEROPONICS, AND AQUAPONICS: These growing methods don't use any soil at all! Instead, plants are grown in water or air. As a result, plants take up less space, can be grown indoors, and use less water. (Food grown using the aeroponics method uses 95 percent less water than plants grown in a field.)

So what can you do? You might think about becoming a farmer or scientist who uses some of these new solutions. You can also make choices right now that influence how food is produced, including these:

Learn about the food you eat. Read labels and know where your food came from and how it was made. Knowledge is an important first step in making better-informed choices.

Eat locally. Shipping food from far away creates excess pollution and waste. Are there foods grown closer to where you live that you can buy?

Try something new. Food that's grown in eco-friendly ways is often more expensive. If that's not in your family's budget, can you try one new thing that was grown in an eco-friendly way, such as organic tomatoes or lettuce from a hydroponics farm?

INTO THE WILD WORLD

I hope the people and stories in this book have shown you just how wondrous our wild world is. And I hope they've shown you how today's environmental challenges can be met with creativity, teamwork, and hope. Reading a book like this is just the beginning. If you're ready to explore and protect our world's habitats, revisit the Field Trip and Stewardship sections in each chapter. Here are some other ways to learn more.

Mountains

LEAVE NO TRACE CENTER FOR OUTDOOR ETHICS lnt.org

Forests

PLANT-FOR-THE-PLANET plant-for-the-planet.org

ARBOR DAY FOUNDATION arborday.org

NATIONAL WILDLIFE FEDERATION nwf.org

Deserts

PROTECT OUR PUBLIC LAND protectourpublicland.org

THE NATURE CONSERVANCY'S CARBON FOOTPRINT CALCULATOR nature.org

Polar Lands

THE WILDERNESS SOCIETY wilderness.org

UNITED NATIONS MAJOR GROUP FOR CHILDREN AND YOUTH unmgcy.org

Ocean

THE OCEAN CLEANUP theoceancleanup.com

SEA LEGACY sealegacy.org

OCEAN CONSERVANCY oceanconservancy.org

Freshwater

RAIN GARDEN INFO epa.gov/watersense/what-plant

Cities

AUDUBON NATIVE PLANTS DATABASE audubon.org/native-plants

Rainforests

KIDS SAVING THE RAINFOREST kidssavingtherainforest.org

Grasslands

AMERICAN PRAIRIE RESERVE americanprairie.org

Other Resources

NASA CLIMATE KIDS climatekids.nasa.gov

NATIONAL GEOGRAPHIC KIDS kids.nationalgeographic.com

ROOTS AND SHOOTS rootsandshoots.org

BIBLIOGRAPHY

Here are the main sources the author consulted while researching and writing this book.

Chapter 1: Mountains

"Bad Reputations." Series 2, Episode 5 of *David Attenborough's Natural Curiosities. Aired March 8, 2014, on Eden (UK).*

Carrington, Damian. "Mountain Gorilla Population Rises about 1,000." *Guardian* (UK), May 31, 2018.

Tabei, Junko. *Honouring High Places: The Mountain Life of Junko Tabei.* Calgary, Alberta, Can.: Rocky Mountain Books, 2017.

4 Wheel Bob. Directed by Tal Skloot. Tritone Media, 2016.

Chapter 2: Forests

Leopold, Aldo. *A Sand County Almanac.* New York: Oxford University Press, 1949.

Lorbiecki, Marybeth. *Aldo Leopold: A Fierce Green Fire.* Guilford, CT: Globe Pequot Press, 2004.

Forest Man. Directed by William Douglas McMaster. Polygon Window Productions, 2013.

Maathai, Wangari. *Unbowed.* New York: Alfred A. Knopf, 2006.

Meine, Curt. *Aldo Leopold: His Life and Work.* Madison: University of Wisconsin Press, 1988.

Parker, Laura. "Teenager Is On Track To Plant a Trillion Trees." *National Geographic*, March 7, 2017.

Sengupta, Somini. "Restoring Forests Could Help Put a Brake on Global Warming, Study Finds." *New York Times*, July 5, 2019.

Chapter 3: Deserts

Adams, Ansel. *Ansel Adams: An Autobiography.* New York: Little, Brown; revised ed., 2017.

Conrad, Tracy. "How Minerva Hamilton Hoyt saved Joshua Tree park for future generations." *Desert Sun*, May 11, 2019.

Harris, G.G., & Cohen, H. *Women Trailblazers of California: Pioneers to the Present.* Charleston, SC: History Press, 2012.

Minerva Hamilton Hoyt (U.S. National Park Service). Retrieved from https://www.nps.gov/people/minerva-hamilton-hoyt.htm.

Netburn, Deborah. "How a South Pasadena matron used her wits and wealth to create Joshua Tree National Park." *Los Angeles Times*, February 14, 2019.

Welts Kaufman, Polly. *National Parks and the Woman's Voice: A History.* Albuquerque: University of New Mexico Press, 2006.

Zarki, Joseph W. *Images of America: Joshua Tree National Park.* Charleston, SC: Arcadia, 2015.

Chapter 4: Polar Lands

Murie, Margaret. *Two in the Far North*. New York: Knopf, 1962.

Niven, Jennifer. *Ada Blackjack: A True Story of Survival in the Arctic*. New York: Hyperion, 2003.

"The Refuge: Fighting for a Way of Life." YouTube, uploaded by Patagonia, November 16, 2018. youtube.com/watch?v=A4DH5cK37Y8&t=30s.

Chapter 5: Ocean

Dance, Amber. "These corals could help survive climate change—and help save the world's reefs." *Nature*, November 27, 2019.

Drabble, Margaret. "Submarine dreams: Jules Verne's Twenty Thousand Leagues Under the Seas." *New-Statesman*, May 8, 2014.

Evans, Arthur B. "Jules Verne." Encyclopedia Britannica Online. April 23, 2020.

Mittermeir, Cristina. *Women of Influence: Cristina Mittermeir*. YouTube, uploaded by B&H Photo Video, March 8, 2017. youtube.com/watch?v=By_etUznKHU.

Potts, Mary Ann. "Unblinking." *Adventure Journal*, Fall 2019, pages 56–69.

Slat, Boyan. "How we will rid the oceans of plastic." YouTube, uploaded by The Ocean Cleanup, May 14, 2017.

Wollerton, Megan. "Cristina Mittermeier is fighting climate change, one photograph at a time." Retrieved from cnet.com/features/cristina-mittermeier-is-fighting-climate-change-one-photograph-at-a-time.

Chapter 6: Freshwater

Douglas, Marjory Stoneman. *Marjory Stoneman Douglas: Voice of the River*. Englewood, FL: Pineapple Press, 1987.

Mapp, Rue. "Creating a New Narrative of People and Nature." *TEDxYosemite*, February 22, 2016.

Mapp, Rue. "Interview of the Week: Rue Mapp." *Our Daily Planet*, February 13, 2020.

Mapp, Rue. "Mentors: Rue Mapp." YouTube, uploaded by The North Face, November 14, 2018. youtube.com/watch?v=eO_URz2PEn4.

Mapp, Rue. "Rue Mapp: Where Black People and Nature Meet." YouTube, uploaded by City of Des Moines, November 26, 2018. youtube.com/watch?v=DhZcOTi2_nA.

"The Swamp: Nature Never Surrenders." Directed by Randall Maclowry. *American Experience*, WGBH, 2019.

Chapter 7: Cities

Finley, Ron. "A guerrilla gardener in South Central LA." TED, March 6, 2013.

Frederick Law Olmsted: Designing America. Directed by Lawrence Hott and Diane Garey. Hott Productions, 2014.

Lopez, Steve. "In the weeds of bureaucratic insanity there sprouts a small reprieve." *Los Angeles Times*, August 20, 2011.

Martin, Justin. *Genius of Place: The Life of Frederick Law Olmsted.* Cambridge: Da Capo Press, 2011.

Scattergood, Amy. "In the dirt with Ron Finley, the Gangsta Gardener." *Los Angeles Times*, May 19, 2017.

Chapter 8: Rainforests

Cullis-Suzuki, Severn. "Severn Cullis-Suzuki at Rio Summit in 1992." YouTube, uploaded by We Canada, August 16, 2012.

"Margaret Mee and the Moonflower." Directed by Malu De Martino. E.H. Films, 2013.

Mee, Margaret. *Margaret Mee's Amazon: Diaries of an Artist Explorer.* Woodbridge, UK: Kew, 2004.

Parker, Laura. "Greta wasn't the first to demand climate action. Meet more young activists." *National Geographic*, March 25, 2020.

Suruí, Almir Narayamoga, & Corine Sombrun. *Save the Planet: An Amazonian Tribal Leader Fights for His People, the Rainforest, and the Earth.* CITY: Schaffner Press, 2018.

Chapter 9: Grasslands

Kimmerer, Robin Wall. *Braiding Sweetgrass: Indigenous Wisdom, Scientific Knowledge and the Teaching of Plants.* Minneapolis, MN: Milkweed Editions, 2013.

Kimmerer, Robin Wall. "Reclaiming the Honorable Harvest." TEDxSitka, August 18, 2012.

Hersey, Mark D. *My Work Is That of Conservation: An Environmental Biography of George Washington Carver.* Athens: University of Georgia Press, 2011.

"George Washington Carver." *Enyclopedia Britannica Online.* Accessed July 24, 2020.

"Where the Buffalo Roamed: Restoring the American Serengeti." YouTube, uploaded by Princeton Conservation Society, October 11, 2018.

Yeh, James. "Robin Wall Kimmerer: 'People can't understand the world as a gift unless someone shows them how." *Guardian*, May 23, 2020.

INDEX